Washing the
DISCIPLES' FEET

Washing the Disciples' Feet

Vignettes of White Oak Original Free Will Baptist Church of Bladenboro, North Carolina

George G. Suggs, Jr.

iUniverse, Inc.
Bloomington

Washing the Disciples' Feet
Vignettes of White Oak Original Free Will Baptist Church of Bladenboro, North Carolina

iUniverse books may be ordered through booksellers or by contacting:

iUniverse
1663 Liberty Drive
Bloomington, IN 47403
www.iuniverse.com
1-800-Authors (1-800-288-4677)

Because of the dynamic nature of the Internet, any web addresses or links contained in this book may have changed since publication and may no longer be valid. The views expressed in this work are solely those of the author and do not necessarily reflect the views of the publisher, and the publisher hereby disclaims any responsibility for them.

Any people depicted in stock imagery provided by Thinkstock are models, and such images are being used for illustrative purposes only.
Certain stock imagery © Thinkstock.

ISBN: 978-1-4620-4124-4 (sc)
ISBN: 978-1-4620-4125-1 (ebk)

Printed in the United States of America

iUniverse rev. date: 08/04/2011

In memory of my parents, George and Carrie Suggs, Longtime Members of White Oak Original Free Will Baptist Church

CONTENTS

ILLUSTRATIONS

PREFACE

To live in Bladenboro, North Carolina during the thirties and forties was to live in the shadow of churches, all of them Protestant denominations in one form or another. Whatever direction one took from the town's solitary stoplight hanging over the intersection of Highway 211 and Highway 242 at the center of town, one was certain to encounter shortly thereafter a house of worship. And on several side roads off these highways near town, the same was true. Within a radius of six to eight miles from Bladenboro, there were numerous churches that served the area population. Churches were seemingly everywhere. Had it been possible for these religious edifices to be suddenly eradicated, the structural architecture of the town and its immediate environs would have been radically altered. The presence of so many sanctuaries in such a small area suggested not only great religious diversity in doctrinal substance and ritual among the residents, but it also suggested the presence of a people whose character was formed and then guided by profound religious belief and faith.

It was my good fortune to have grown up in White Oak Original Free Will Baptist Church located less than a half-mile west of town. From my birth in 1929 until I entered Wake Forest College (now University) in 1947, unless circumstances prevented our attending services there—such as the illness of my mother, inclement weather, or lack of transportation when we lived in distant homes—Sunday morning found the Suggs family worshiping at White Oak. (Its members usually referred to their church simply as White Oak and not by its full name.) Prior to her marriage, my mother and other family members had long been members there, and not long after her marriage to my father in 1927, he also became a member. Consequently, until my departure for college, White Oak was my church "home" and its members were my church "family." Later, as a teenager I, too, became a member after I had responded to an altar call during a revival meeting led by Rev. Walter Jernigan and after my baptism in June Singletary's millpond.

Not long ago, my thoughts began to turn more frequently to White Oak and the former members of its congregation, most of whom are now gone on to their reward. It's not that I had not thought about the church in the many intervening years since my transfer of membership from the church and the Free Will Baptist denomination. Quite the contrary. For rarely do I attend any Protestant religious service, regardless of the denomination, when I am not reminded—in some manner (usually by the singing of hymns)—of my youthful years at White Oak.

The more that I have thought about my formative years in the church, the more I realize what a profound influence its members, its services, and some of its leaders had on my over-all personal development, spiritual and otherwise. The membership included many members of my extended family (almost exclusively on the maternal side), so that attending services on Sunday morning was like a large family reunion. Included on the church rolls also were a half-dozen or so fascinating personalities who often and unexpectedly enlivened the on-going proceedings that made services interesting for other members of the congregation. Furthermore, the fiery sermons by ministers—whose energetic efforts to preach the Word and the necessity of being "born again" sometimes left them wet with perspiration, and whose sermon content rested almost solely not on formal, institutional study of the Scriptures but on divine, spiritual inspiration and revelation—certainly kept the attention of young people like myself. For youngsters, their descriptive views of heaven or hell as the ultimate outcome of one's life journey were frightening indeed. But it was the music, the wonderful hymns that we sang, that had a tremendous impact on my spiritual journey. Even today when I hear some of these old songs, so full of faith, theology, and spiritual yearnings, sang in my present church, my mind flashes back to hearing them as a boy being sung by the congregation of White Oak, the words and music conjuring up personal, spiritual emotions and even the facial expressions of some of the members as they sang.

No one could grow up in a church like White Oak without being impacted in both positive and negative ways. Institutions have that effect on the young. In my case, the impact was mostly positive. Not only were my parents part of White Oak's religious influence on my life, but there were other wonderful people in the congregation who also helped to shape my spiritual journey and helped to make me into who I am. A few of them are mentioned in the vignettes of church life that follow, vignettes that are meant to be a tribute to them. A reader should keep in mind that this work is a book of reflections, impressions, and memories. It is not designed to be a documented history of White Oak Original Free Will Baptist Church. On the contrary, it is only one person's recollections of his experiences and observations of life in the church during his youth. Someone else will have to perform the task of a formal history. Consequently, others who were members of the church while I attended there may have memories that differ substantially from mine. And that is as it should be, because perceptions by individuals invariably differ concerning people and events commonly shared and experienced. Of course, individuals with memories in conflict with those expressed here are free to present their own.

CHAPTER 1

The Congregation

For as we have many members in one body, and all
members have not the same office: So we, being many,
are one body in Christ, and every one members one of
another. Romans 12: 4-5

As noted earlier, White Oak Church was located on Highway 211 less than a half-mile west of the town of Bladenboro and about the same distance east of the Bladenboro Cotton Mills. Like the West Bladenboro Baptist Church, the nearby Church of God, the Fire Baptized Holiness Church, and other churches close to the mills, the membership at White Oak was composed principally of textile workers and their families. It is likely that when the original church was built about 1917 on land donated by Latt Edwards, closeness to the mills and the company's two mill villages (the Old and New mill "hills"), where so many of its members worked and lived, was an important factor in determining its location. Furthermore, in the absence of widespread car ownership, choosing a location for the church within easy walking distance of the bulk of the membership was a rational choice. For as long as I was a member of the congregation, White Oak Church in character was essentially a working-class church consisting of members drawn from the mills. Of course, there were a few farm families and representatives from other occupations, but without the large component of mill hands and their families, it is unlikely that the White Oak Church would have existed.

By far the largest and most influential family within the membership of the church was that of Daniel Edmund and Excie Hester, my maternal, great-grandparents. (I have used the spelling "Excie" found on her tombstone rather than the often used "Exie.") Daniel and Excie had eleven children (Bob, Blaine, Seth, George, Jim, Rachel, Tine, Celia, Mary Ann, Elery and Fannie), all of whom, with the exception of daughters Tine, Mary Ann, Fannie, and son Elery, who died early, lived within a half-mile of the sanctuary. Most of them were mill workers. Dan Edmund, as he was called, was a legendary figure who was among the church's founders. Although he died in 1936 when I was six or seven years old, while growing up I often heard stories about his great devotion and faithfulness to the church, how on cold winter mornings he always fired up the big pot-bellied, coal stove before the service in order to warm the building for the congregation, how it was he who also took responsibility for ringing the church bell to call the members to worship, how he displayed remarkable and constant patience and love for Excie despite her irascible and ill-tempered nature, and how he somehow survived living with five devilish sons whose temperaments were more like Exie's than his own. Following his death, the congregation honored him by hanging his picture on the church wall. Many church members, including my mother (a granddaughter), considered him truly saintly in character.

On Sundays, the children and spouses, grandchildren, and great grandchildren of Dan Edmund and Excie nearly filled White Oak Church, which was not a very large sanctuary. After the death of Dan Edmund, Bob, the second oldest of his sons, became the acknowledged leader of the Hester clan. He and his wife Maybelle, who lived within sight of the church on Highway 211, had eight children, three sons and five daughters (R.J., Eddie, Mary Eliza, Ozell, Leona, Juanita, Lydia Mae, Thelma Lee) who, until they matured and left home for either military service or marriage, attended regular services at White Oak. Even after marriage, some of them continued to attend services, their growing families swelling the membership. Maybelle, the wife, was the exception. A rather private person, her attendance was infrequent. Tobacco-chewing Bob, who had risen to a supervisory position in the Old Mill (Mill No. 1), appeared to provide guidance in church matters to all his siblings, all of whom were members. His influence on church finance, on the "calling" of a preacher for the monthly sermons, and on the general affairs and operations of the church were enormous. For example, if he decided that the congregation should select a specific minister to preach, it seemed that the rest of the Hester clan usually fell in line and supported his choice. While I was growing up in the church, therefore, Bob was probably its most powerful member because of his influence on his siblings and their family members who made up the bulk of church membership. Even as a youth, I became aware that his role in the church often had a very great impact because regardless of his position on issues, some of which were very divisive, his children, siblings and their children tended to follow his leadership. However, there were a few of Dan Edmund and Excie's grandchildren who did not blindly follow Bob's leadership.

Bob's brother Jim and his wife Molly also helped to fill the pews of White Oak Church. Like his brother, Jim was a longtime worker in the Bladenboro Cotton Mills, and, like his brother Bob's family, Jim's family did not live on either of the mill villages. They occupied a residence across the Seaboard Railroad and Bryant Swamp and adjacent to what was known as the Bridger field, which was within easy walking distance of the church and mills by way of foot-logs across the Bryant Swamp. During Jim's time in the mills, safety was not a major concern of management. Not only was the air saturated with lint that made workers more susceptible to tuberculosis and brown lung disease, but the machines, powered by an overhead system of gears and leather belts, were extremely dangerous to work around. Unfortunately, Jim was badly injured when an arm was caught in a belt and pulley system. Nevertheless, after healing, he returned and continued his work in the mills. It was rumored that in the absence of financial compensation for his injury, Jim was guaranteed lifetime employment in the mills.

Jim and Molly produced eight children (Allie, Ellery, Clyde, Ferris, Warren, Miles, James, and Marie) who became members of White Oak and regularly attended until they moved away. In time, some of the children filled leadership roles in the church. For example, for years Ellery was treasurer and kept track of the institution's finances. I remember his frequent financial reports to the congregation, and the presence in church of his wife Maryline and their two children. And when the new sanctuary was built, for awhile Warren was chosen to be in charge of the building fund, receiving and dispensing funds involved in construction. Jim and Molly's other children regularly attended church functions such as Sunday School and preaching services. Of the eight children who remained in the immediate area, upon marrying and having offsprings of their own, like Ellery they took their place in the congregation. This was true of sons Clyde, Ferris, and Warren.

George was another of Dan Edmund and Excie's sons who worked in the mills and, like his older brother Bob, George attained a lower-level supervisory position there. George and wife Fannie also had a substantial family of seven children (R.D., Maxine, Jeanette, Edwin, Michael, Jerry, and Ashley) who attended White Oak Church while growing up. R. D. left the family early and enlisted in the U. S. Army where he remained until dying of a heart attack. I don't recall much about Maxine and Jeanette and their participation in the activities at White Oak. They were older than I. As I recall Edwin was somewhat of a loner who went his own way, and the other three brothers, who were younger than I, do not provoke many memories in connection with White Oak Church.

Blaine was another of Dan Edmund and Excie's children. Unlike the other family members, Blaine worked hard at finding other lines of employment than mill labor, principally in sharecropping and peddling fish in the mill villages. He and his wife Georgia produced five children (Kathleen, Pauline, Curtis, Eugene, and Jesse), all of whom—except Jesse who died as a youngster after eating contaminated sardines—regularly attended White Oak Church.

Like most of his other brother siblings, Seth worked in the local cotton mills with his wife Evelyn. Of Dan Edmund and Excie's sons, Seth's family was the smallest, producing only two children (William and Lois Jean). For many years they lived on a nearby mill village within easy walking distance of the church. Although not the most active and visible members of the Hester clan in church activities, his family nonetheless helped to augment the influence of the Hester family in church affairs. Sometime during the thirties (1937-1938), my family and Seth's family shared a rented house on the Old Mill village, which allowed me to know Seth better than some of the other Hester brothers. I remember Seth and Evelyn as good people. Seth died of a heart attack while mowing grass.

The female children of Dan Edmund and Excie also helped to swell the congregation of White Oak. Fannie, who married Charley Edwards, had six children (Marybelle, Carrie, Lu, Naomi, Woodrow and Boyd) before dying at age forty-nine of a stroke in 1926. Two of the girls, Marybelle and Carrie (my mother), were strong, active members of the church. Each of them married a mill worker, Carrie to George G. Suggs and Marybelle to David J. Pait, and as a consequence, lived near the mills and the church. In the early thirties Carrie's and Marybelle's families shared a rented house on the Old Mill village. Each had two children who were active participants in nearly all church activities until marriage and military service took them away from the congregation. I don't recall that the other four children of Charley and Fannie Edwards were ever members of White Oak Church, instead, joining other churches in the area, such as Mt. Calvary that was also a Free Will Baptist Church.

Rachel, another daughter of Dan Edmund and Excie, with her husband Leland Shipman also belonged to White Oak Church. The Shipman's had three offsprings (Leo, James, and Vivian) who attended on a regular basis until departing home for military service or marriage. Rachel and her family lived within sight of the church across Highway 211 from her brother Bob. Because of the proximity of the two families, there was much interaction between them, especially following the death of Dan Edmund when Excie moved in with Rachel's family. Furthermore, in summer Rachel's front porch was often a Sunday afternoon gathering place where the extended family of Hesters gathered to talk about church and other subjects. It was here that I think that Bob, acknowledged leader of the Hester clan, probably exerted his enormous influence on the clan's thinking about the internal affairs of White Oak Church. Porch conversations would last into the evening, making it necessary for Rachel to set out smoke pots to fight off the hordes of mosquitoes invading from nearby Bryant Swamp.

Mary Ann, the most frequently married of the Hesters, was also a member of White Oak Church, except in those years when she moved away to be with one of her three husbands. While married to her first husband, a man by the name of Davis, she had a son name Roy. Mary Ann attended the church principally in her later years when she moved in with Roy and his wife Ruby following the deaths of her husbands. The Davis family, who were also mill workers, had five children (Fred, Richard, Frankie, Jo Anne, and Victor). Fred, was struck by a car and killed on Highway 211 in September, 1941. Ruby, a very devout woman, was principally responsible for having her family in church on Sunday morning. The family's presence helped to swell the number of people in the congregation who were direct descendants of Dan Edmund and Excie.

Had daughters Celia and Tine remained in Bladenboro, their offsprings would have swelled even more the Hester influence on White Oak Church. Nevertheless, even without the these two sisters and their families, the progeny of Dan Edmund and Excie substantially filled the pews during many church activities, especially Sunday morning services.

Another important family in the membership was that of Rev. H. C. and Hattie Adcox who lived adjacent to White Oak Church. A retired minister, Rev. Adcox exercised enormous influence in church proceedings, frequently serving as moderator in church elections and other events, and often joining with Bob Hester in pushing certain issues in the church such the choice of ministers, the building program, and so on. He and Hattie had seven children (Stella, Esther, Mella, Dorothy, J. C., and Walter) who attended church until dispersed out of town by marriage and work. Unfortunately, another son was killed when struck by a car near a railroad siding running into the cotton mill. Like her husband, Hattie was a leader among the women of the church, actively participating in the Ladies Aid Society, denominational conferences, and general church affairs. Because of the background and activities of Rev. Adcox and his wife, and because they lived adjacent to the sanctuary, their children were usually in church whenever the doors opened. Like the Hester family, their numbers also swelled the attendance because all or some of the family were always present when church was in session.

Although not possessing as many children, there were other families that were extremely important in the life of the church. Among them was the Graham and Ada Wilson family that consisted of only three members. The Wilsons had only one child, Marie, who was their pride and joy. Early in her youth, Marie became convinced that God was calling her into foreign missions and she obeyed that call. Although her decision left the Wilsons without their daughter following high school when she went off to Marion College in Indiana, they nevertheless sacrificially accepted her decision as the will of God. Until his death about 1945, Mr. Graham (as he was called) was a moral force within the church, and Mrs. Ada (as she was called) continued to be so until illness restricted her attendance by confining her at home. There was no one in the church more respected than the Wilsons whose lives reflected their deep faith. My family and others were the recipient of many favors from the Wilsons who were always ready to help when needed. Mr. Graham was one of a very few members who were not connected in some way with the cotton mill. However, he worked as the lead clerk in dry goods in the largest mercantile establishment in town, the Bridger Corporation, that was owned by owners of the mill.

Sam and Mittie Edwards were also important in the life of the church. It was Sam's father who gave the land upon which the church was built. Like so many others, they worked in the nearby cotton mill and lived in the Edwards family's old home place, which Sam had inherited from his father Latt, in close proximity to White Oak Church. The Edwards had two children, Sydney and Annie, who were my contemporaries while growing up. As youths, Sydney was one of my closest friends and remained so until his death in his fifties. A high-strung, nervous woman, Mittie nevertheless frequently joined the ladies in the work of the church. As for Sam, who was an extremely intelligent man, he impressed me as someone who constantly questioned much of what he heard coming from the pulpit at White Oak. He was something of an agnostic. The Edwards were good friends of our family, a friendship that lasted until their deaths. Members of the Edwards family regularly attended religious services.

Directly across Highway 211 from Sam and Mittie Edwards lived Sam's brother Bud and his wife Magdalene. With their son Tommy, they also attended White Oak Church, Magdalene and Tommy more so than Bud who seemed to have other interests. Magdalene was a very obese, peppery woman who sometimes made interesting and humorous remarks during church proceedings, for example, at the election of the preacher for a coming term. Until the late forties when they built and operated a small store near the highway, Bud and Magdalene worked in the nearby cotton mill. Unlike his brother Sam, who was a rather thoughtful, quiet man, Bud was a renowned storyteller who frequently regaled his fellow workers—and later his customers—with tall tales. I don't recall Bud attending church as much as his wife.

Eddie Johnson and his wife were faithful members of White Oak Church. The Johnsons had two children, a daughter named Christine and a son whose name I do not remember, perhaps because he was younger than I. Like so many other members who attended White Oak Church, Eddie and his wife worked in the cotton mill. They did not reside on the mill village but in a small house off Highway 211 within easy walking distance of the sanctuary. Although not actively involved as leaders, I recall that they were usually present on Sunday mornings and that their children participated in church sponsored activities for the youth.

Another faithful family that attended White Oak Church was that of Willie Bowen. He and his wife had two daughters, Merle and Hilda. A rather short, plump man who was known for his fishing ability, Willie was also a textile worker whose family lived off the mill village and near enough to the church to easily walk the short distance for services. Merle and I were in the same class in the Bladenboro Public Schools; Hilda, her older sister, was a year ahead. And at White Oak, we, together with other children our age, were often in the same Sunday School classes. From time to time, Willie held minor offices in the church. The Bowen family members were among the most reliable when it came to attending services. They were one of the core families of the church.

David Hester and his family were also an important asset to the church. Unlike most of the other adult members who worked in textiles, the Hesters lived several miles out of town and were farmers. David and his wife had several children, all of them older than I. I remember that one of them was called Graham. I remember him because my middle name is Graham and while a youth, I was also called by that name. David was one of the leaders at White Oak Church. As I recall, he was elected to serve as Sunday School superintendent on several occasions. He had a deep, resonant voice and a conspicuous Adam's apple that moved up and down when he talked or sang. When he wasn't superintending, he was a member of the Sunday morning group that formed the "choir." The Hesters had sons in the service during World War II, as did several other families in White Oak Church, for example, the Shipmans and the Hesters. I remember a heartfelt, public prayer that David once gave in behalf of his and other members' sons of the church facing dangers abroad during the war.

Kelly Pait, who was related in some way with Ada Wilson, was a bachelor who lived out of town on a farm. Kelly, whose idiosyncracies caused some members of White Oak Church to think of him as being "strange," traveled to Sunday services by bicycle on Sunday morning, weather permitting. Sometime during the late forties, Kelly apparently despaired of the single life and solved his problem by ordering a wife through a mail order catalogue. When she arrived by train on the

Seaboard Line with her children, Kelly, now with his new, ready-made family, continued to attend services. Kelly's marriage thus increased the size of the congregation by several members. He apparently found happiness with his new wife and her children.

Bliss Hester and his wife lived toward town on Highway 211 within easy walking distance of the church. Bliss, who was a carpenter, had a large family of boys and girls, none of whom, as I remember, ever attended services at White Oak Church. Or, if they did so, they did not attend on a regular basis. As young adults, Bliss's sons were particularly hard for him to control because their life-styles were so in contrast with his. Like David Hester, Bliss was elected by the congregation several times to serve as Sunday School Superintendent. While I was a member, he was one of the more active members the church. I remember his standing before the congregation on Sunday mornings conducting the proceedings before the start of classes.

Another family that I recall attending White Oak Church was that of Cecil and Flora Bennett who also worked in the cotton mill. However, Cecil later became a small time entrepreneur, operating at different times two small stores on Highway 211 and, later, a another near what was then known as the "New" mill. His customers were principally mill workers. The Bennetts had two sons, Lester and J.C. Like Sydney Edwards, J. C. was one of my best friends. The Bennetts were not regular in their attendance, particularly Cecil, who seemed to have other interests.

Cornelia Gainey, a widow, was a very active member of the church. She and her son Raymond resided on Highway 211 in close proximity to the sanctuary. Cornelia earned her living working in the cotton mill. Like other women in the church, from time to time she taught youngsters in Sunday School. And I remember that she and my mother infrequently sang duets accompanied by my Aunt Marybelle Pait on the piano. Raymond, who was a year older than I, was a good friend who attended church regularly with his mother. As discussed elsewhere, when the congregation decided in the late forties to build a new sanctuary, the Gaineys' purchased the original church for its lumber. I helped Raymond dismantle part of the old church.

Mary Storms and her husband Grad were also members of White Oak Church. Grad was a carpenter and Mary was a housewife who was among the more active women in the church. They had no children, but sometime in the late forties they took in a teenager named Junior Kinlaw. I don't remember ever seeing Grad at church, but Mary always attended services. With other women she taught Sunday School classes, and with my mother and my Aunt Marybelle was involved in leading the children's choir. On occasions, she was the church pianist.

Two other members come to mind—Harry Pait and LeRoy Brown. I am not sure about the marital status of Harry. I remember that he regularly attended Sunday morning services alone. LeRoy, his wife, and daughter lived several miles from the church on the Dublin road. Like so many other church members, he worked in the mill. He and his daughter attended but on an irregular basis.

Undoubtedly, there were other members of White Oak Church who are not mentioned in this brief survey of the congregation as it existed during my formative years of the thirties and forties. If I have failed to mentioned any family, it is the result of the failure of memory. Leaving for military service in 1951, I was never again an active member. However, my parents remained members until the mid-fifties, and when visiting home, I attended services with them. There were certainly changes that occurred in the membership during the immediate years following my departure. So, it should be noted my observations apply only to those years that I actively participated in services there. And, it should be further noted, that memory is fallible and often unreliable.

Nevertheless, several conclusions seem reasonably accurate. As repeatedly noted, most of the members of White Oak Church were workers in the Bladenboro Cotton Mills. If there was ever a working-class church, this church was one during my involvement there. Work in the mills provided a common experience that created a sense of community among the majority of its members, a sense that contributed to a general understanding of the troubles and hardships they mutually suffered during an era of depression and war. The members were linked not only by a common background in the secular world of work but also by their interpretation of the Christian faith espoused by the Free Will Baptist denomination, which has been discussed elsewhere. For the members of White Oak Church, work and faith were part of the cement that bound them to each other. Occasionally they might disagree and squabble over church issues, but in most cases these episodes were short-lived because of their awareness of community.

Another linkage that bound the members together was the fact that nearly all the members were related by blood or marriage. During the thirties and forties, it would have been nearly impossible to find anyone in White Oak Church who was not directly or indirectly related in some manner to everyone else in the congregation. As noted above, the Dan Edmund and Excie Hester offsprings were the dominant family in the church; however, the genes of Dan Edmund and Excie were spread throughout all the membership. For example, my mother was one of their numerous grandchildren. The genealogical links were astounding; the family interconnections hidden in obscure layers of bloodlines and marriage. Consequently, when the congregation met for services, it was very similar to a large family reunion of close and distant relatives, with a few outsiders (for example, my father and David J. Pait) who were thrown into the family mix by virtue of marriage. So, work, family and faith formed at times a near homogeneous—yet sometimes volatile—mix on Sunday mornings. For relatives in extended families often experience disharmony as well as harmony as they mingle closely together in whatever activity they are engaged in. So it was at White Oak Church.

An unfortunate characteristic of the congregation was the lack of education among its members. If there was then anyone of the older generation in the church with a high school education, I am not aware of it. Toward the end of my membership there, an older grand-and/ or great grandchild of Dan Edmund and Excie occasionally made it through the local high school, but the generation of my parents, aunts, and uncles was poorly educated—through no fault of their own, to be sure, but nevertheless, poorly educated. For example, my mother, who had been forced to leave high school while in the tenth grade to care for a younger sibling, went back to finish while in her fifties, and then went on to take college courses at Pembroke State College.

But the prevailing expectation—even among many mill hands—was that the children of cotton mill workers were destined for the mills and, consequently, there was no need for much formal education. Education was not a high priority. Not all church members held this view (for example, my parents), but I think that the majority felt this way. This unfortunate attitude toward education was another link binding many members of White Oak Church into one big family.

CHAPTER 2

Washing the Disciples' Feet

He riseth from supper, and laid aside his garments; and
took a towel, and girded himself.
After that he poureth water into a bason, and began to
wash the disciples' feet, and to wipe them with the towel
wherewith he was girded. John 13:4-5 KJV

While growing up as a member of White Oak Original Free Will Baptist Church, one of the most interesting religious rituals I participated in was that of washing the disciples' feet. This ritual is not practiced in most mainline churches today, probably because washing another member's feet is a truly humbling experience (not many of us are humble anymore), and getting down on one's knees with a towel and a basin of water at the unshod feet of another person to perform such a menial, servant's task lacks the sophistication that most worshipers have come to expect in today's religious services. Consequently, most major denominations have dispensed with the practice, their ministers discreetly avoiding scriptural references that seem to call for it. For example, I have been a member of a local United Methodist Church for over forty years without ever observing a session of feet washing by its members. However, there is a scriptural basis for the practice of washing feet as a religious ritual, and the few churches that adhere to the practice claim that they do so because it is commanded in the Gospel of John.

Following his triumphal entry into Jerusalem riding on an ass, Jesus and his disciples made preparation for the feast of the Passover. According to the Gospel of John, Jesus knew then that the meal he would eat with his principal followers would be his last meal with them. He was aware that the time had come for his forced departure from this world. In his description of the Last Supper (John 13: 4-17, KJV), John, his beloved disciple, relates a feature of Jesus' final meeting with the twelve disciples that writers of the other gospels failed to mention, that is, the washing of the disciples' feet and the significance of the act in explaining his—and afterwards theirs—servant role.

Unexpectedly, Jesus stood up from the meal, removed his outer garments, wrapped himself with a towel, poured a basin of water and began to wash the disciples' feet, explaining to them that, although they might not understand then why he was performing such a menial task, they would understand later. None raised an objection to having his feet washed until it became Peter's turn. Stating that he would never allow Jesus to wash his feet, Peter adamantly refused until Jesus told him that unless he permitted his feet to be washed, he could never be a part of God's kingdom. Hearing that remark and fearing the consequences of further refusal, Peter acquiesced, telling Jesus to wash not only his feet but also his hands and his head. Afterwards, Jesus removed the towel, re-clothed himself with his outer garments and again sat down at the table and taught them the meaning of his surprising action. He said: "13. Ye call me Master and Lord: and ye say well; for so I am. 14. If I then, your Lord and Master, have washed your feet; ye also ought to wash one another's feet. 15. For I have given you an example, that ye should do as I have done to you. 16. Verily, verily, I say unto you, The servant is not greater than his lord; neither he that is sent greater than he that sent him. 17. If ye know these things, happy are ye if ye do them."

As part of the Original Free Will Baptist denomination that literally interpreted this passage from the Gospel of John as a commandment that should be followed, the members of White Oak Church practiced foot washing while I was part of the congregation, believing that in doing so, they were obedient to the example that Jesus gave to his disciples. In other words, they were "feet-washing Baptists" who followed, as Biblically instructed, the example of their Lord to wash "one another's feet." As I recall, the members of White Oak Church did this at least once a year.

While a part of White Oak's congregation during much of my early childhood, because there was no reason for me to do so, I paid little or no attention to the church's ceremony of feet washing initiated by Jesus and recorded in the Gospel of John. This was a ritual followed by older members of the congregation. It was not until following my conversion, baptism and becoming a formal member of the church as a teenager that I first noticed and engaged in the practice when it occurred. Even then, however, I don't recall participating in the ceremony but once while a member of White Oak. One of the beautiful things about the Free Will Baptists was their emphasis on "free will." And I must confess that after becoming a member I often exercised my "free will" not to wash another member's feet and have that member wash mine. As a teenager, the practice did not appeal, perhaps was even odious, to me. The very notion of washing someone's dirty feet was very repugnant to me. (Not until later did I discover that members came to this ritual with very clean, freshly washed feet.) At the time, I did not comprehend the extraordinary message that Jesus conveyed by that simple, humbling act. My resistance against the practice was strong enough to negate the strong encouragement by my parents that as a Christian I ought to do so. Even so, I do remember a time when I allowed myself to be persuaded to humble myself enough to join my parents and others for a session of foot-washing. It turned out to be quite an enlightening experience.

At the time—as I recall it was sometime in the early Spring during the war years of the early nineteen forties—the White Oak congregation then occupied its old wooden sanctuary that was heated by a huge pot-bellied stove located in the front of the building. The night was very cold and the stove, though fiery red, seemed to be throwing off very little heat, certainly not enough heat to be felt in the two Sunday school classrooms that had been added some years earlier as an annex to the original building. The feet-washing service that I was part of occurred on a Wednesday evening (or it might have been on a Maundy Thursday), an evening that was ordinarily set aside for prayer meetings. Probably because of the cold weather, there were not very many worshipers who attended this meeting. Following a brief prayer service with Communion led by the Reverend H.C. Adcox, a short, white-haired, elderly man, that focused on the verses in the Gospel of John describing the Last Supper and the washing of the disciples feet by Jesus, those present then separated by gender, the men moving off into the left annex, and the women retiring to the right annex, rooms that were ordinarily classrooms. For obvious reasons, in these services men and women did not intermingle when washing feet.

It was immediately evident that there had been prior preparation for the meeting in which I participated. A church-owned stock of galvanized wash basins was available for the ceremony but the towels, if I am remembering correctly, were brought by the worshipers. From a modern viewpoint, except for electric lighting, the old White Oak Church structure was then a primitive facility that lacked all the modern conveniences common to today's churches. For example, it had no indoor plumbing, that is, there was no indoor access to water and thus no indoor access to toilet facilities. Drinking water for the congregation was obtained from an outdoor artesian well (we called it an "overflow") that constantly produced a stream of pure, cool, potable water that was delicious. A two-seat outhouse located at the back of the church building provided the only toilet facility for use by the congregation.

This absence of modern conveniences impacted both on the service of washing feet and other church activities. For example, prior to the feet-washing meeting a church member had collected water from the overflow in foot tubs and placed them in the annex for later use by the worshipers. Even in the summertime, water from the overflow was always extremely cool and thus pleasant to drink. Collecting the cool water and storing it on a chilly evening in an even colder church building some distance away from its stove—even a large, hot stove—with a limited heating range did little to warm it for later use. It actually became colder as it sat in the wings of the building awaiting its use.

At this particular session of feet washing, as I recall, there were approximately a halfdozen men and myself who adjourned to the left annex to wash each other's feet in commemoration and obedience to Christ's example. Perhaps it was the cold environment of the room, or, maybe my own distorted, teenage expectations about the occasion, but I expected the event to be a very solemn occasion. Paradoxically, there seemed to be neither the solemnity nor the seriousness that I expected to find in the service. Once in talking about his experience in a previous service, my father, who could always find something humorous in most situations, had laughingly related that while down on his knees washing the Rev. Adcox's feet, a large, angry looking wasp had dropped from the ceiling onto one of the reverend's big toes. It had left my father with a temporary dilemma of what to do—slap the wasp off the toe and risk having the preacher stung, or, simply sit and wait until the wasp voluntarily decided to buzz away. He never told that story without laughing about Rev. Adcox's startled reaction when he became aware of the wasp sitting and flexing his stinger on the nail of his big toe. Fortunately, the wasp flew away and no harm was done to the reverend's foot, but the story should have suggested to me that washing the disciples' feet was not without its humorous moments, that it was not an entirely serious and somber occasion.

A possible explanation for the lack of high seriousness that I observed was that with one or two exceptions, the men that evening were good, close friends who worked together in the local cotton mill, and they probably found some humor in the ritual of washing each other's feet. Kneeling there shivering in the coldest part of the church while washing a member's feet in very cold water generated some humorous comments from some of the men concerning the cleanliness or lack thereof of a friend's feet. All of them, however, had done what I had done before the service. They had thoroughly washed their feet to avoid this criticism. And most had put on their very best socks for the occasion. Under the circumstances, this particular feetwashing session did not last very long. The very cold room and the use of very cold water undoubtedly led to a speeding up of the ceremony, for shortly after separating into the annexes, both men and women soon collected around the big pot-bellied stove trying to warm up. Afterwards, following a song and prayer, we left the church and went out into the night.

I don't think that the innocent humor expressed by the men during the feet-washing ceremony, undoubtedly provoked by sticking their feet in a basin of cold water, denigrated in anyway the seriousness with which the participants considered the proceedings. The very presence of the men and women in the service testified to their belief that in washing a fellow member's feet, they were following the example of Jesus. Furthermore, I believe that they thoroughly understood the lesson that Jesus taught his disciples during the Last Supper when he humbled himself as a servant and washed his followers' feet. Consequently, I readily discount the lack of high seriousness among those church members who participated in the service. The people involved were good Christian people who followed their faith to the best of their ability. I feel certain that their innocent repartee with each other during the ritual was not offensive to the one whose example they were attempting to follow. As for me, it was an experience that I have never forgotten. Each time I now read the above passages from John, I recall that episode of washing the disciples' feet.

CHAPTER 3

Prayer Meetings

Be careful for nothing; but in everything
by prayer and supplication with thanksgiving let your
requests be made known unto God.
Philippians 4:6 KJV

Wednesday evening was the time for prayer meeting at White Oak Church. As long as I remained a member there, this time was set aside for the more faithful and dedicated members of the church to meet and pray about personal problems, problems within the church, problems in the nation and the world, and whatever problems happened to be on their minds that made them feel the need for prayer. The nineteen thirties were depression years and times were economically hard for all members of the congregation. I do not remember anyone at White Oak who prospered during those bleak years when unemployment soared, jobs were both hard to find and keep, and wages were abysmally low. Furthermore, the early forties were war years when a number of young men from the church were drafted into the armed forces and served overseas in major combat theaters. For example, my mother's people, who made up much of the church membership, had a number of sons, husbands, and brothers (for example, my mother's brother Boyd Edwards) in harms way, a fact that influenced the content of many prayers at the weekly Wednesday meetings. Consequently, with depression and war prevailing during the thirties and the forties, there was much for members of White Oak to be anxious about and much to pray about. And being devout people who believed in the efficacy of prayer, they did not hesitate to take—as a hymn writer has penned—their "burdens to the Lord and leave them there."

Prayers meetings at White Oak did not attract many worshipers. The number usually participating in the service was approximately a dozen or so. I don't think that this was because the absent members of the congregation judged the service unimportant, or, that they were any less faithful or devout than those who attended. Many of the absentees would have attended had they been able to do so. There were practical reasons they did not participate. Very few members of the church had automobiles during this period. The times were hard and few members, most of whom worked in the Bladenboro Cotton Mills, could not afford cars. Within the church, there may have been less than a half-dozen who were fortunate enough to afford automobile ownership in those hard times. Furthermore, during the war rationing of tires and gasoline forced them to use these vehicles sparingly, sometimes forcing a choice between Sunday services, prayer meetings, or more secular activities.

As a result, for most members without transportation, walking was the only means of getting to White Oak for all religious services, but especially for the Wednesday evening prayer service. Furthermore, for those who walked, weather was sometimes a hindrance. The ones who regularly attended, therefore, were those who lived within easy walking distance of the church. Among them were members of the George Suggs and the H. C. Adcox families—both of whom lived adjacent to church property. Members of other church families who lived nearby on or near Highway 211 also infrequently attended. These included members from the Hester families of Bob, Blaine, Jim, Seth, George, Rachel, and Maryanne, and the families of David James Pait, Grad Storms, Eddie Johnson, and Cornelia Gainey. Sam and Mittie Edwards, and Leroy Brown were car owners who sometimes attended; Graham and Ada Wilson were nearly always there. Most of those attending the Wednesday prayer services, with a few exceptions, were connected either by marriage (for example, my mother was related to nearly everyone in the congregation, especially the Hesters), or, by work-related experiences in the cotton mill. So to a large extent, the meeting provided an opportunity for a small group of relatives and others to socialize, to discuss family matters, conditions in the mill, news about sons in the war, and, of course, to pray. During the winter, the small prayer group usually gathered around the pot bellied stove for warmth. As described elsewhere, White Oak Church was a wooden structure with a high ceiling and tall windows, making it a very difficult

19

sanctuary to warm solely with a stove, even a large one. On cold meeting nights, the worshipers hovered around the stove until the service began. And in the summer time, the windows were raised as high as possible to take advantage of any breeze that might be available. Of course, with the church being located adjacent to Bryant Swamp, open windows often invited in hordes of mosquitoes, which resulted in much slapping at the pests and caused some discomfort.

As I recall, there was not much structure to most of these prayer meetings, that is, structure in terms of defined leadership or someone being permanently in charge of the sessions. The proceedings were rather informal, but the service always involved Scripture reading, singing, praying and testifying. The proceedings invariably began with a prayer. Rev. Adcox, a retired minister who lived next door usually gave the opening prayer, the group deferring to his status as a minister and his age. However, Mrs. Ada Wilson, who could render beautiful, but long, public prayers was sometimes asked to make the opening prayer. It was customary for a hymn to follow. During regular Sunday services, the pianist was someone who had been chosen at the annual election of church leaders. While I was a member, the elected pianist was either Carrie Suggs (my mother) or her sister Marybelle Pait. But at the Wednesday night prayer meeting, it seems that one of these two members played only when Hattie Adcox, wife of the minister, was absent, which was not often. Hattie's playing skills were limited. Her ability to read music was limited to the old-fashioned shaped notes. Consequently, the hymn chosen had to be something within her very inadequate repertoire of church music. And it seems that nearly always—at least when I attended a prayer meeting—her initial hymn of choice was "Work for the Night Is Coming." This was a song that was simple to play and one that everyone seemed to know. I rarely hear this song anymore, but to this day when I hear it, I can picture Hattie banging away on the piano, occasionally pausing after missing a note, as the group sang along, trying to follow as best they could.

Following the opening prayer and song, Scripture was read. Who selected the passage to be read from the King James Version—always the KJV because it was then about the only interpretation available—remains a mystery to me. One of the ladies usually performed the task of reading Scripture because the ladies were by far the better readers in the White Oak congregation, and, consequently, the reader probably made the selection prior to the meeting. Afterwards, the reader led a serious discussion of the meaning the passage and its application to everyday life. As I now look back on these discussions with the advantage of age, I realize how remarkable were the spiritual insights into Scripture revealed in the comments made by some who attended these prayer services, for example, Ada Wilson and my mother. Very few of them had much formal education. Actually, I don't think that any of them had graduated from high school because time and circumstances had prevented an easy access to much formal education. But with their smattering of education, they also possessed great native intelligence, and informed by the Spirit they read their Bibles carefully and thoughtfully, a fact reflected in the points they made and the questions they asked in discussion. Although not theologians, they had a heartfelt grasp of the Scriptures that would make some formally trained theologians envious.

There followed a session of open prayer—the primary reason for the meeting—in which anyone was free to join in if one felt so inclined, or, if "led by the Spirit" to do so. Although a few were hesitant and refrained from participating in public prayer, most of those attending these Wednesday night prayer services readily did so. The content of their prayers reflected their worries and concerns about a variety of subjects—personal health, the spiritual state of a loved one, a faraway son in uniform possibly in harms way while at war, relationships within the family, economic problems, and so on. These prayers were from the heart and were often accompanied by emotion. Typical of these prayers was one by David Hester who, at the time, was serving as Sunday school superintendent and who had two sons in wartime service. One Sunday morning, I recall that he rendered a fervent, emotional prayer pleading with God for divine protection for not only his sons but for all those serving in the armed forces. While down on their knees, worshipers at the Wednesday evening prayer meeting sent up equally fervent prayers that expressed their faith in a loving, merciful, powerful God who, if willing, could answer all their requests.

The prayer session was usually followed by short testimonials about all that the Lord had been doing in their lives. Not everyone was inclined to stand up and testify, but the opportunity was given to anyone to publicly express his faith and to relate some personal experience that revealed God's presence in his life. Some told how through their prayers, God had helped them to resolve problems they could not solve alone. At times they described the problems they had been unsuccessfully wrestling with before turning to God for assistance. Others were silent about their troubles, but they requested prayers that God, who knew "all about my worries," would intervene to help. There were some who testified about blessings they had experienced, and they wanted to publicly express their thankfulness to God for his grace and presence in their lives. Occasionally, testimonials were humorous. My father told of one such occasion.

Norman Hilburn, who was a friend, was an off-and-on preacher who had conducted a revival meeting at a country church in nearby Columbus County. Once during an evening service while Norman was preaching, several drunks entered the church and proceeded to disrupt his sermon which, of course, he naturally took exception to. Later, the local authorities were notified and the men were arrested, jailed, and convicted of disturbing a religious service. Their conviction naturally created animosity toward Norman because of his role in having them imprisoned. As a result, they allegedly sent him a threatening message that if they ever again found him in that part of the county, they would kill him. Norman took the threat seriously and he refused other invitations to preach at the church. The threat continued to prey on his mind, causing some troubling friction between him and his wife who downplayed the incident and apparently nagged her husband about his childish fear concerning the threats on his life. She wanted him to return to the church and preach.

During the course of a prayer meeting at White Oak where he was a member, while testifying Norman told the assembled group about the episode in Columbus County and about his wife's harassing him about his fear of returning there. He reportedly quoted his wife as saying to him in a critical way, "Why don't you go back and preach in that church, you old coward? If you don't go back there and preach, that's what you are—an old coward." Her comments sorely hurt the preacher, so much so that he sought prayerful help from his fellow worshipers. According to my father, after Norman related his concerns about how his wife had badgered him over his fears, he reportedly justified his refusal to confront the potential threat to his life in Columbus County by saying, "Bless God, I'd rather be a live coward than a dead hero!" In telling about this worrisome episode in his life, Norman, of course, was prepping the group to remember him in their prayers. Although his testimony was humorous because of the way he presented it, Norman nevertheless revealed his deep faith in the efficacy of prayers by his fellow believers in his behalf which, in closing, he asked for. Such humorous episodes were definitely the exception in the Wednesday evening prayer services.

Following the period of testimonies, the service usually ended with a song. Anyone attending could suggest the closing hymn. However, if Hattie were at the piano, she had the final say-so because the song had to be one that she could play. Sometimes it was necessary to offer several selections before finding one that she felt comfortable enough to manage. I don't recall a hymn ever being sung acapella. After the closing hymn, the service always ended with a prayer, often offered by a volunteer, and a brief break-up social gathering before everyone departed into the night for home.

I think that the Wednesday night prayer service was an integral part of the religious life at White Oak Church during my membership there. Although a low percentage of the congregation usually attended, for the members who did the service was extremely important. Perhaps because our home was adjacent to the church, my parents were among those who regularly attended the services. My mother, who for years experienced health problems, always found the prayers and testimonials at these meetings very comforting to her. I am certain that the same was true for others who attended. In some denominations, the traditional Wednesday prayer service has gone by the wayside. Modern life with its many distractions make humble kneeling and praying to God—even one evening a week—seem either an unusual burden or a terrible waste of time. It was not so at the White Oak Church that I attended during my formative years.

CHAPTER 4

Faith Healing

Is any sick among you? Let him call for the elders of the
church; and let them pray over him, anointing him with
oil in the name of the Lord. And the prayer of faith shall
save the sick, and the Lord shall raise him up . . . .
James 5:14-15 KJV

In the kind of world we live in today, it is difficult to find many
individuals who openly and unconditionally believe in faith healing,
except, of course, among the members of evangelical denominations
who remain true believers in the power of prayer to bring about even
miraculous spiritual, physical, and mental healing. It seems that the
science of modern medicine and a dominant scientific world view have
fundamentally undermined reliance on faith as the best means to restore
wholeness of soul, body, and mind. That reliance has also been undercut
by films such as "Elmer Gantry" that exposed the ability of shyster
ministers to exploit people of faith for profit by the use of trickery
and subterfuge. Furthermore, the many examples of exploitation by
unscrupulous ministers out for gain that have been revealed over the
past years through the media of radio and television have also reduced
the number of persons who believe in the power of faith and prayer to
bring about wholeness. Whatever the general status of this belief now
is, it was at the time of my attendance at White Oak Church a strong
article of faith among its "born again" members and throughout the
Free Will Baptist denomination.

If one reads in the New Testament about the many miracles
performed by Christ during his short ministry, one can easily understand
why professing and devout Christians at White Oak Church would
embrace the possibility of divine healing. Restoring sight to the blind,

curing horrible diseases such as leprosy and other afflictions, returning the crippled to mobility, restoring sanity to the mentally ill, raising the dead—these miracles plus others that revealed to believers Christ's control over all natural phenomena were convincing evidence of His power to heal if it were His will to do so. In reading their Bibles, Free Will Baptists found that in nearly every episode of healing recorded there, the element of faith or a strong belief in Christ's divine power to heal was present in the person restored to wholeness. Furthermore, other scriptural passages convinced them that if their faith was strong enough, they could move mountains, and that any request made in the name of Jesus, believing, would be granted. And there were other passages that instructed them that if any believer among them was ill, that person should call upon his elders to pray for and to anoint him with oil because the prayers of the righteous were said to be heard in heaven. Many members of White Oak Church, including my parents, fervently believed in these Biblical episodes of divine healing and the scriptural promises about the power of prayer for the sick.

Unfortunately, it was the strength of this faith in divine healing that made so many Christians, including some at White Oak Church, unusually vulnerable to the practice of charlatans who instinctively understood how to exploit for gain the vulnerabilities found in the powerful combination of faith and desperate human needs, both physical and mental. Furthermore, there were many believers who out of simple ignorance or lack of education were extraordinarily susceptible and fell prey to the appeals of such ministerial quacks who claimed special access to godly powers to address and cure human frailties. However, unlike Christ, who never accepted rewards for his merciful and compassionate acts of healing, these unscrupulous preachers had no reluctance to milk innocent believers dry by playing on their faith. In doing so, when exposed they frequently undermined the humble belief of the faithful.

My mother, who was an ardent believer in the power of prayer to heal, conditioned, of course, on it being God's will, once related a story of observing a minister at a revival meeting whom she suspected of exploiting the strong but simple faith of many worshipers in the congregation. Following a fiery sermon and an altar call, the minister asked any person with physical problems to come forward for anointing with oil and praying to be healed. My mother, who had a lifetime heart problem, dutifully went forward with other believers, among whom was a man she did not know who claimed to be suffering from a mouthful of bad teeth. Although there was much fervent praying at the altar by the preacher and others for the afflicted, there were no astonishing miracles that occurred that evening. However, during the testimonial period at the next meeting of the revival, the person with the allegedly bad teeth revealed what was tantamount to a miracle, stating that overnight his bad teeth had miraculously disappeared and had been replaced with a mouthful of wonderful gold teeth that he refused to display to confirm his claim.

Thereafter, my mother, an intelligent woman, always believed that the recipient of the alleged miracle had been planted among those attending the revival meeting. That questionable episode of divine healing, however, never undercut her strong faith in the promises of the Bible concerning the power of prayer among "born again" Christians. I witnessed the strength of her faith on a number of occasions, but I remember one incident in particular that demonstrated her strong religious beliefs about prayer and that also expressed the relevant doctrines concerning prayer of the Free Will Baptist denomination to which White Oak Church belonged.

After being stricken with rheumatic fever while a teenage girl, a disease that left her with a damaged mitral valve of the heart, my mother was subject to periodic cardiac "spells"—a "racing," a "fluttering," and/ or "pounding" heart, irregular beating, etc.—that convinced her that her death was imminent. Understandably, such episodes tremendously frightened her, causing her to fall back upon her religious faith and her doctor for help and comfort. I remember that as a teenager, my mother's "spells" not only generated anxiety in her but also in me and other members of the family who also feared that she was near death. A visit by our family doctor, Dr. Dewey H. Bridger, usually calmed her fears, but there were occasions when his presence and prescriptions did nothing to alleviate her anxiety. It was at such times that she drew strength from her faith in the Biblical promises that was part of her denomination's creed. During one of these unusually disturbing "spells," I saw her faith in the power of prayer put to the test. I am certain that something similar occurred to other members of White Oak Church when they too confronted illnesses that were life threatening.

As recall, my mother had been ill and bedridden with a severe "spell" of the heart when she requested, following the instructions to the sick found in the Book of James, that the deacons (elders) of White Oak Church come to our home, anoint her with oil, and pray for her recovery. Her request was consistent with her strong, personal belief in the power of prayer and, of course, consistent with the belief of her denomination. I believe that such requests from sick members of the White Oak congregation were expected by the religious leadership, because once as a boy I had occasion to be behind the pulpit of the church and I saw there a small vial of oil, possibly olive oil that had been blessed by prayer, that I understood was used for anointing the sick. Following her request, several members of the church and family members led by retired minister H. C. Adcox gathered in my mother's bedroom, and after anointing her forehead with oil, we all knelt on our knees around her bedside, and prayed fervently for her recovery.

There was no immediate, miraculous healing of my mother as result of the prayers that evening. Her heart condition did not disappear. Until her death approximately thirty-five years later, she continued to have "spells" with her heart that required constant medical care. However, following the prayer session described above, her health gradually improved to the point that although her physical activities were limited, she remained active and involved in the life of White Oak Church. Through the years, I watched how her faith pulled her through one medical crisis after another, for example, several blood clots thrown off by a fibrillating heart, anyone of which could have killed her instantly. With each episode, her faith grew stronger, so much so that even after being told by her doctor that her fibrillating heart would one day throw off a clot that would kill her, she continued to place her full trust in the power of God to forestall that event. I am convinced that her belief in the power of prayer sustained her through many trying experiences caused by bad health.

In thinking back about various members of White Oak Church, I am certain that there were others in the church who held fast to their belief in faith healing, just as my parents did. Devout people like Graham and Ada Wilson, Rev. H. C. and Hattie Adcox, Ruby Davis (later known as a "prayer warrior" because of the power of her prayers), my Aunt Marybelle, Mary Storms, and Cornelia Gainey impressed me with the strength of their faith in the power of prayer.

I don't mean to suggest that there were not others equally devout. Nor do I mean to suggest that these members were more righteous or holier than others. They are just a few who immediately come to mind. Because of the hard times of depression and war they were forced to endure, the members of White Oak Church certainly had much to pray about. It was fortunate that they belonged to a denomination whose doctrines never questioned the power and efficacy of prayers made by righteous people, and they never discounted the possibility of miracles if God so willed. The belief in the power of prayer and the belief that with God all things were possible marked the congregation as I knew it.

CHAPTER 5

Revivals and Baptisms

Halelujah! Thine the glory,
Halelujah! Amen;
Halelujah! Thine the glory,
Revive us again. P. MacKay & John J. Husband

Not long ago, while viewing for the third or fourth time a movie entitled "Oh Brother! Where Art Thou?" a scene in this film reminded me of a ritual that was of great significance in the life of White Oak Church. In the film three escapees from a Mississippi chain gang were warily resting in a wooded area near a river. Their reverie was suddenly broken by the sound nearby of choir-like singing of "Down to the River to Pray" coming through the trees. Upon investigating the source of this heavenly music, they discovered a line of singers clad in robes similar to white bed sheets moving slowly and ghost-like down toward the river bank where a baptizing was in progress. One of the escapees, who obviously was experiencing inner turmoil because of his predicament in fleeing from the law, was unusually moved by the religious ritual and music, so much so that he broke from his fellow escapees, raced fully clothed to the water's edge, waded out to the preacher standing waist deep in the water, interrupted and broke into the line of new converts awaiting baptism, and demanded immediate immersion. The minister obliged, delighted, I suppose, at this unexpected convert who had raced from the trees with such evident enthusiasm to participate in this ritual of salvation. Emerging from the water dripping wet, the newly baptized convict joyfully shouted to his two friends on shore that he had been "saved" and all his sins had been "forgiven." In his mind, his spiritual salvation had also freed him from his previous felony convictions. A fellow convict, the most intelligent of the three, could not convince

29

him otherwise. Watching this scene from the movie, I was reminded of the baptisms that I had observed at White Oak Church, particularly my own baptism.

In the evangelical churches in Bladenboro and the surrounding area, it was customary to have a revival meeting either in the Spring or the Fall of the year. The purpose of these meetings was to "revive" the religious life of church members already "saved," to return "back-sliders" to the fold, and to reach out to "lost" sinners and bring them to salvation. These meetings usually lasted for a full week, or, depending on the circumstances, they might be extended for another week. That is, if there was a sense of inadequate revival or an awareness that there were some sinners outside the fold, perhaps loved ones, who were teetering and tottering on the brink of conversion, the revival would continue. In these meetings, it was extremely important that the "lost sheep," whether within the church or out, be given every opportunity to seek forgiveness for their sins and to accept and embrace salvation before it was "too late." For believers, these revival meetings were an extremely important part of the religious life of the church and community. This was certainly true at White Oak Church.

At a minimum, a revival at White Oak involved a full week of preaching and singing when the focus was on producing a greater commitment of current members to Christ and his teachings and reaching out to persons who were deemed to be eternally lost, trying to persuade them that the time was ripe for their salvation if they wished to escape an eternity of hellfire and damnation. From my observations, this outreach at White Oak was directed principally to the younger members of families who were entering their teenage years and were judged to be unusually vulnerable to the sins of dancing, picture shows, sexual promiscuity, and other sinful activities. In other words, the youth who had not yet made a firm, religious commitment and become members of the congregation were the principal targets of the revival. Nevertheless, the net was cast far and wide enough to include sinners who fell under the mesmerizing power of preachers who did not hesitate to strike the fear of God into their listeners with vivid descriptions of an eternity of hellish, endless suffering if they failed to accept God's grace and be saved because they refused to seek forgiveness for their earthly sins.

These revival services did attract local sinners—persons who really needed to change their way of life—and others who were just looking for a way to spend an evening. For example, some teenage friends and I heard of a revival meeting underway at the Fire Baptized Holiness Church, which was situated at the north end of the Old Mill village. This church was known for the way the Spirit moved among its congregation. For some reason—probably the possibility of meeting up with young ladies or simply curiosity—we decided to attend a revival service. When we arrived the service was well underway, the preacher already having worked up a sweat and a growing hoarseness from his vigorous movements around the pulpit and his loud preaching. His actions and verbal description of what awaited sinners if they failed to seek forgiveness and come to Christ was even then having a visible effect on his listeners, many of whom were being gripped by the Spirit as evidence by their rising voices and physical motions. Shortly after the preacher ended his sermon and extended the altar call, a number of already agitated men and women began raising both hands to heaven, shouting, and speaking in "unknown tongues." Emotionally overcome, several women lay writhing on the floor while praising the Lord, completely oblivious to their surroundings. When some of the "saved" began circulating and attempting to persuade people in the audience to come to the altar, my friends and I slipped out the back door of the church. It was a memorable experience.

The revival services at White Oak Church never reached the extreme emotional pitch that my friends and I witnessed at the Fire Baptized Holiness Church. I do not recall seeing at White Oak anyone ever shouting, speaking in tongues or writhing on the floor in some form of ecstasy while a service was in progress. This is not to say that revival services there lacked emotion, for they indeed did. Mothers, including my own mother, were genuinely concerned about the "lost" status of their children, and in their desire to encourage the salvation and entrance into heaven of their offsprings, they would often leave their seats and pressure their children to seek forgiveness at the altar. Once there, a reluctant son or daughter was quickly surrounded by parents, several passionate church members and the preacher who prayed fervently for the salvation of his lost soul.

All the while the congregation or choir was repeatedly singing "Softly and Tenderly," "Just As I Am," "Why Not Come to Him Now?" "Why

Not Tonight," "Jesus is Calling," or other songs imploring reluctant sinners to leave their seats and come forward. Mixed in with the music were frequent exhortations from the minister begging and pleading with the hesitant and reminding them of what eventually awaited them if they did not—that is, to be eternally lost in hellfire and damnation. For many teenagers like myself, the atmosphere during these revivals was tense and emotional caused by mixed feelings of not wanting to disappoint concerned parents, being frighten by the possibility of an eternity in hell as described by the preacher, and worrying about what one's peers might say—the possibility of ridicule—if one went forward in response to the altar call. For the young like myself who were resisting the pressures to go forward, the preacher's altar call seemed to go on forever, particularly verses of the hymn "Just As I Am." I remember that the night I went forward to the altar, I was conflicted by such concerns.

As I recall White Oak Church was having its Fall revival that was led by the Reverend Walter Jernigan. Jernigan was a homegrown preacher who had felt the "call" when he was a young man, and he had served as pastor of the church from time to time. He was a likable minister who, I remember, had visited my mother once in a Lumberton hospital. Concerned about her failing health, she had expressed her concern that she might die from her heart condition. According to my mother, who when telling about the visit often laughed, Jernigan trying to relieve her concern had said, "Well, Carrie. We're all gonna die sometime of something." At the time that was not what she wanted to hear. She wanted his prayers for her recovery. However, she later found his statement full of truth and humor. (Jernigan later proved the truth of his statement when he dropped dead of a massive heart attack on Front Street in Bladenboro.) But on the night I went to the altar with some encouragement from my mother, Jernigan had preached a fiery sermon in which he graphically described all the terrible consequences that would befall any listener who failed to heed his warnings that then was the time for repentance and salvation.

As the congregation sang verses from "Just As I Am" over and over again at the instruction of Jernigan, I recall growing more and more uneasy, especially as I saw my mother looking at me with a pleading look. I knew that she wanted me at the altar as a means of assuring her that should she die, we would most certainly be together again in heaven.

Furthermore, there were ladies moving about the church encouraging loved ones to step forward to be saved. I recall fighting the impulse to leave my seat, but, then to my surprise, I found myself moving forward to join a few of the unsaved at the altar where I soon found myself in spiritual turmoil as prayers, mixed with tears, went up in my behalf. It all finally came to an end when the congregation recognized by hugs and handshakes the new converts who had had their sins washed away by the blood and were now on their way to heaven. It was after this experience that my baptism occurred.

Like most of the churches in Bladenboro, White Oak did not baptize its new converts within the sanctuary. It lacked the facility to do. Consequently, like the river baptism in "Oh Brother Where Art Thou?" the church's baptisms were conducted outdoors in streams or ponds. In my case, the site chosen for this important religious ritual was June Singletary's mill pond that was located several miles out of town off the road to Dublin. At one time this large pond was the site of a grist mill, but by the decade of the forties it had fallen into a mere relic of by-gone days. Its basic structure stood but nothing else. Nevertheless, from the pond a steady stream of water poured over its dam, dropping down the mill race into a much smaller basin below that was additionally fed by a small stream. Here the very cool, tea-colored water was shallow with a sandy bottom on one side, but on the other side next to a large cypress tree, the water was very deep and covered in shade. In the summer, the deep side was mostly used for swimming by local boys. Sydney Edwards, a close friend, and I frequently rode our bikes there for that purpose. And as teenage Boy Scouts, our Troop 72 often camped there at different times of the year. It was a lovely site to spend a summer afternoon swimming and dropping from a swinging rope suspended from the cypress into the cool, clean water. The shallow side with is sandy bottom was an excellent place for baptisms.

On a Sunday afternoon following the revival in which I was "converted," a dozen or so members of the congregation, the preacher, my parents, and perhaps several other converts gathered below the mill dam on the bank near the shallow water. My mind was awhirl and blurred with emotions. About all I specifically remember prior to baptism was that something significant and important to my life was about to happen and the anticipation was nerve racking. I don't remember how the family got to the baptismal site because we had no car. Perhaps we went out in Graham Wilson's car. He was one of the few members who had a vehicle. Before the baptism, there was singing by the group, but I don't remember the hymns that were sung. There were prayers, but I don't recall who made them. There were people there whom I had known all my life, but I don't remember anyone other than my parents and Walter Jernigan, the preacher who had led the revival and who was to immerse the converts. I do remember the baptism itself.

When the time came to be immersed, the reverend, except for shoes fully clothed, waded out into the water up to his waist and one by one the new converts joined him in the water. Having swam in the pond, I fully expected the water to be very chilly. However, the moment I stepped barefooted, ankle-deep into the gritty, sandy bottom I began a frightful shivering that I then attributed more to the Spirit than to the coldness of the water. It seemed that I had never before been in such frigid water. As I watched Jernigan fully immerse the converts ahead of me in a graceful dipping motion, baptizing them "in the name of the Father, the Son, and the Holy Ghost" after repeating their names, my shivering seemed to grow worse. And then it was my turn! Standing in front of the preacher and trembling like a leaf in the wind, I was now in waist-deep water with only a portion of my shirt still dry. Instructing me to hold my nose tightly, turning me sideways, and placing one hand behind my head and other under my arm, he said my name and baptized me "in the name of the Father, the Son and the Holy Ghost." Whether from the Spirit or being completely submerged in the cold water, I felt a shock run through my shaking body. Like the escaped convict in "Oh Brother! Where Art Thou? as I surfaced and waded back toward the church members standing on shore, I sincerely felt that all my sins had been forgiven! I was truly "born again"! The ritual ended with congratulations and prayers. In the brush I dressed into dry clothes and left the scene with my parents.

I suppose that everyone, especially youngsters like myself, who has undergone baptism in a June Singletary-mill-pond kind of natural setting emerged confident that something truly remarkable even miraculous had happened that transformed soul and mind, making one into a completely changed person, a "new being in Christ" as the apostle Paul wrote. I waded from that chilly water believing all the preacher had said during his fiery revival sermons. That is, by walking to the altar one night I had somehow embarked on a path that was ultimately to save me from an eternity of hellfire and damnation as my mother used to say when someone asked from what had she been saved when she accepted Jesus as her savior.

My baptism formally made me a member of White Oak Church whose members continued to have a major influence on my life until I left them to become part of another congregation. I am certain that my experience was duplicated many times and helped to constantly replenish the membership of the church. Among the indelible impressions left by my regular attendance at White Oak was the day I was baptized by Walter Jernigan in that small reservoir behind the dam of June Singletary's mill pond.

Today, the area described above has been reconfigured so that it is very different. A substantial bridge has been built over the creek that flowed into the baptismal pond, making it possible for one to look down on the site. The remnants of the grist mill have been removed from the dam. But still standing is the cypress that provided so much excitement for boys who, when swinging from a rope, could drop into the deep side of the pond and plunge into that cold, cold water and daringly seek the bottom. No one knows how many churches used the small pond for baptisms, but I imagine that many did. It is unlikely that June Singletary ever refused a church's request for such use.

CHAPTER 6

Children at White Oak

Praise Him, Praise Him, all you little children.
God is love. God is love.
Praise Him, Praise Him, all you little children.
God is love. God is love. Children's chorus.

Although possessed with very limited resources, White Oak nevertheless played an extremely important role in developing character and religious sensitivity in the children who attended its services. Nowadays, many churches are so blessed with abundant financial assets that children's ministries form an integral part of church life. Services directed at children now encompass a broad range of activities directed by ministers who have been specifically trained to work with young people. In an effort to attract and keep the children involved in the church, such youth ministers are found in most large mainline churches where they are a vital part of all church life affecting youth.

As in all modern life, religious specialization has become an essential part of spreading the good news. Because persuading the young to the Christian way is an absolute must if churches are to survive and grow, work that used to be done with youth by devout members of the congregation has now become the responsibility of a professionally trained youth leader. This was not so at White Oak Church during the thirties and forties. It was difficult enough to pay the preacher for bi-monthly, or sometime, a monthly preaching service. There was no money for a resident pastor or parsonage much less for a youth specialist. Besides, no one in the church had ever heard of a minister whose job it was to work solely with the youth. Thus involving young people in the life of the church was the accepted responsibility of lay members who willingly volunteered their services.

The most outstanding example of lay members' work among the children was in the field of church music. When a child in the congregation reached school age, he was encouraged to participate in the children's "choir" that was a part of every Sunday morning service. This was an impromptu, informal group sing that had no organizational structure and no prior practice sessions. At the appropriate time, children were asked to come forward to the front of the church where they sat on straight-backed chairs awaiting direction from the director, always a lady member who might differ from Sunday to Sunday.

There were several ladies who assumed the task of teaching the youngsters simple choruses full of religious content. None of them had had any formal musical training in working with youth—other than the fact, of course, that most of them were mothers with children attending White Oak. Among these women were my mother, my Aunt Marybelle Pait, Cornelia Gainey, and Mary Storms. My mother and Aunt Marybelle, sisters who more or less alternated in being annually elected church pianist, were always involved in playing the piano for the children's choruses. If either one was not at the piano, the other, more than likely, would be serving as the director of the choir. In the absence of one or the other, Mary Storms or Cornelia Gainey would be called upon to fill in to lead the children in a range of choruses. As a boy who was encouraged to march forward every Sunday to sing in the "choir" (I had no choice because my mother would not take no for an answer.), much to my surprise I found that I enjoyed singing along with the other children. None of us had much talent; however, the little choruses that we learned at the prompting of these ladies have endured in memory for a lifetime. The music was simple and the words seemed to stick.

Among the choruses whose words and melodies I remember so very well—and I am sure others who were there remember them, too—are among the following.

Jesus Loves Me

Jesus loves me, this I know,
For the Bible tells me so.
Little ones to him belong,
They are weak, but he is strong.

Yes, Jesus loves me. Yes, Jesus loves me.
Yes, Jesus loves me. The Bible tells me so.

Jesus Wants Me for a Sunbeam

Jesus wants me for a sunbeam, to shine for him each day.
In every way try to please him, at school, at work, at play.
A sunbeam! A sunbeam! Jesus wants me for a sunbeam!
A sunbeam! A sunbeam! I'll be a sunbeam for him.

Jesus Loves the Little Children

Jesus loves the little children, all the children of the world.
Red and yellow, black and white, they are precious in his sight.
Jesus loves the little children of the world.

This Little Light of Mine

This little light of mine, I'm going to let it shine.
This little light of mine, I'm going to let it shine.
Let it shine, let it shine, let it shine.

Praise Him, Praise Him

Praise him, praise him, all you little children.
God is love, God is love.
Praise him, praise him, all you little children.
God is love, God is love.

Deep and Wide

Deep and wide, Deep and wide,
There's a fountain flowing deep and wide.

Deep and wide, Deep and wide,
There's a fountain flowing deep and wide.

Climb, Climb up Sunshine Mountain

Climb, climb up sunshine mountain, heavenly breezes blow.
Climb, climb up sunshine mountain, faces all aglow.
Turn, turn, from sin and Satan, climb into the sky.
Climb, climb up sunshine mountain, you and I.

Little Hands Be Careful

I washed my hands this morning,
So very clean and bright.
I gave them both to Jesus,
To work for him 'til night.
Little hands be careful,
What you have me do.
Anything for Jesus,
Only let me do.

Into My Heart

Into my heart. Into my Heart.
Come into my heart, Lord Jesus.
Come in today. Come in to stay.
Come into my heart, Lord Jesus

Fishers of Men

I will make you fishers of men, fishers of men, fishers of men.
I will make you fishers of men, if your follow me.
If you follow me! If you follow me!
I will make you fishers of men, if you follow me.

Everybody Ought to Love Jesus

Everybody ought to love Jesus,
Jesus, Jesus.
He died on the cross
To save us from our sins.
Everybody ought to love Jesus.

Of course, the children did not sing all these choruses every Sunday. Usually, whoever directed the choir selected only several to sing. My mother and Aunt Marybelle could easily play by ear on the piano whatever choruses the director chose. As the young singers grew older they left the group, became part of the congregation, and joined in singing regular hymns. They were replaced with younger children who filled the seats of those who left, so that there was a constant stream of children into and out of the choir. Without practice and learned, musical leadership, our performances naturally lacked the polish and sophistication of other children's choirs that I later observed. However, the children at White Oak gained an appreciation for religious music as they were gradually integrated into the life of the church.

As one might expect in looking at the content of the choruses, the religious content is evident and consistent with the doctrines of the Free Will Baptist denomination. The concept of God's love and the nature of that love is clearly identified, as well as the expectation that, if a Christian, one's life was supposed to reflect that love. Furthermore, clearly evident in some of the choruses is the further expectation that one should avoid sin at all cost, and that in all things one should see the hand of God and constantly praise him. In looking back on my participation in the children's choir, it is clear that it was an important method of instilling basic religious concepts into children at a very early age. The ladies who took the time to direct each Sunday morning were not the highly trained individuals that are found directing children's programs in today's modern churches, but they nevertheless were very effective in influencing children in the right direction.

Equally significant in introducing the children of White Oak to the doctrines of the church was its Sunday School. Attending church school on Sunday morning was an integral part of the worship service for all the children who were expected to participate. The same ladies who guided the children in music were the same ones who played the major role in educating the youth of the church on religious matters—my mother, Aunt Marybelle, Mary Storms, Hattie Adcox, and Cornelia Gainey. One of these women taught the youth from preschool through their teenage years. I don't recall ever having a man teacher during my youth at White Oak. The teachers were always women. The only contact with a male Sunday School teacher that I personally had occurred when I attended the men's Bible class, which, of course, was taught by a man.

The distinctions that marked the different classes as we progressed through the Sunday School into our teenage years have become blurred in memory by the passage of time. I do remember that during the preschool years that the church literature was limited to cards with scenes and verses from the Bible containing simple lessons (for example, "God is love") that the teachers tried hard to etch into our developing minds. Later, after we were older and had learned to read, the literature became more demanding and the religious concepts became more sophisticated in that they were supposed to be basic determinants to our behavior as Christians. Other than their personal study of the Bible and their efforts to apply its principles in their own lives, our teachers had little training, that is, formal training in methods of teaching. Their teaching consisted of explaining to the best of their ability what the Scriptures meant and how its lessons should be applied in our lives. Because these women were leaders in just about everything that went on at White Oak, they were listened to with respect, their lives serving as the best lesson of all for their students. They had a thankless job, one that they did to the best of their ability.

Another area of church activity that involved children was the annual Christmas program, which has been discussed elsewhere in some detail. The program always involved an enormous amount of work for those in charge. Like most other activities involving the youth, the same women who directed children's music, summer Bible school, and regular Sunday School for children were also responsible for the Christmas program. They tried to involve as many youth of the church as possible. Sometimes they were successful in doing so; sometimes they were not because some children refused to participate and their parents did not "encourage" them. In any case, the women made a conscientious effort to persuade all the children to participate. Even when they were unsuccessful, the Christmas Eve program drew practically every young person attending White Oak. It was the one event in church life that never failed to attract most of the youth. I think that the principal reason they came was because it was Christmas and even though they might fail to receive a gift from the drawing of names in the Sunday School class, the church traditionally saw that every child present left the service with small paper sack of fruit, nuts and candy. For some children during the depression years of the thirties and the war years of the forties, this small bag of goodies might be all the gifts they received for Christmas. For children from the mill villages, the bag might be an important addition to the Christmas bonus offered by the mill—usually a larger sack of fruit, nuts and candy—to each working family. Although much appreciated by the mill hands, the amount of these items was often very limited.

White Oak involved children in Bible school during the summer. I don't remember but one session in which I participated, but I know that I must have attended others because I have a picture of a group of students and myself standing outside the east end of the church. With few memories of what went on in the summer Bible school, I can only speculate about the program that the ladies offered to their young charges. The focus was obviously on the Bible and supplemented what they were attempting to do in their regular Sunday school classes. From the one picture that I have, it appears that the number of children attending Bible school were few in number. However, from the standpoint of the ladies who were involved, they were doing important work for the Lord whether there were many children or a few.

Compared to children's programs in many of today's churches, the program at White Oak Church would not compare favorably in terms of available resources that could be directed toward influencing youth. However, there is no doubt that many children in the church benefitted enormously from the efforts of devout women with a strong commitment to develop traits of character in young people built around the Christian faith. I believe that collectively they succeeded. Furthermore, individual mothers and fathers aided in this process. For example, my mother constantly encouraged her sons to participate in church activities, easing their way into the full life of the church. Other parents did likewise. In the long run, White Oak Church proved to be a major influence on the lives of many of the children who attended there.

CHAPTER 7

Dinner on the Grounds

And they, continuing daily with one accord in the
temple, and breaking bread, from house to house, did
eat their meat with gladness and and singleness of heart.
Acts 3:46 KJV

One of the most interesting events in the life of White Oak Church was one that did not occur very often—dinner on the ground. It was the practice of the local Free Will Baptist churches to hold quarterly meetings to which churches like White Oak, Mt. Cavalry, Oak Grove, Beaver Dam, and others within the conference would send representatives (usually preachers, deacons, or significant lay members) for the purpose of reviewing and conducting whatever common business there was that affected these churches within the denomination. When held these quarterly conferences rotated among the various churches. Consequently, from time to time each church assumed the responsibility of serving as host to the visiting delegates who would arrive early and generally spend an entire day listening to and giving individual reports concerning activities in their churches, conducting a variety of other business, and worshiping with songs and prayers.

Most of the Free Will Baptist churches in the conference to which White Oak belonged were located in nearby rural areas with no access to commercial lodging or nearby restaurants. Thus it fell upon the congregation hosting the conference, usually held on Saturday, to provide a mid-day meal for their visitors and, in some cases, overnight accommodations. Once when the meeting occurred at White Oak, the decision was made by the ladies of the church to have dinner on the grounds. This was the only such dinner that I remember while a member of White Oak because after its congregation built a new sanctuary in the late forties, meals at the church were served indoors where weather was of no concern.

I recall that the site selected for the dinner was on the east side of the church where there was an open space large enough for temporary tables to be set up. Directly across from the location and separated by a small ditch that ran into Bryant Swamp was my parents' substantial garden where during the summer months, we grew a variety of vegetables that my mother canned for our use during the winter. Immediately adjacent to the dinner site was an artesian well, L-shaped and less than knee high, that was locally known as an "overflow." It flowed night and day, with its water draining into the above mentioned ditch. At that time, the water table in the area was so high that one did not have to sink pump piping very deep into the ground in order to strike a strong, steady head of potable water. White Oak's overflow had a small hole bored in the top of its lateral pipe so that by placing one's hand over its mouth, deliciously cool drinking water squirted up several inches high. The overflow provided whatever water the church needed for rituals like feet washing, cleaning, and drinking. And, until our family was financially able to sink a hand pump on our property, its water also came from this source. Beyond but near the overflow were two beautifully shaped white oak trees just inside the church's property. They were to remain until their removal caused by the construction of the new sanctuary. With no indoor plumbing, visitors to the church dinner found it necessary to use a two-seat outhouse located close by at the rear of the church, discreetly hidden from view behind an annex used for a Sunday school room.

To host one of these quarterly conferences required much preparation, demanding the cooperation of both men and women of the congregation. The ladies of the church met and decided on what foods each was to prepare and bring together with plates, glasses, and utensils. And the men were primarily concerned with the physical facilities that would have to be set up for the outside meal. In each case, individual members had to assume a specific responsibility in order that upon arrival, the delegates from the conference churches would be adequately fed—and in some cases housed for the night. In some respects, preparation for dinner on the ground was similar to preparation for a large pot-luck meal.

For this particular event that occurred in the early Fall when the weather remained warm, my father assumed the responsibility of preparing a tub of iced lemonade for the guests, and my mother volunteered fried chicken. I recall that shortly before the delegates ended their morning session in the sanctuary, the ladies who were not involved officially in the conference began to arrive, usually walking short distances to the church, loaded with their contributions to the dinner, some of which had been prepared the day before. Coordinating our lemonade making with the arrival of the ladies with the food, I began collecting buckets of water from the overflow and pouring it into one of our family's large, galvanized wash tubs that we had carefully scrubbed clean and placed under the two white oak trees. Much earlier, my father had purchased from the company store of the Bladenboro Cotton Mills a dozen or more lemons and sugar, and from the company ice plant a large block of ice that had been carefully wrapped in a croaker sack with sawdust to prevent its melting. Working under the shade of the two oaks, we cut and squeezed the lemons into the water, poured in the sugar, chipped chunks of cleaned ice, and stirred the mixture with the family's wash pot stick, frequently tasting the product to determined whether more sugar or lemons were needed. We wanted it to be just right for the visitors!

Meanwhile, the ladies, while laughing and talking, worked feverishly placing the food on the makeshift tables that the men of the church had earlier set up, scurrying to have it ready when the delegates ended their morning session. Because the times were difficult, the items placed on the table were basic foods such as vegetables from local gardens: peas, beans, okra and tomatoes—homemade biscuits, fried chicken, pork chops, and desserts of pies and cakes. Nevertheless, the women took obvious pride in what they had contributed to fill the tables with delicious and attractive food. After loading the tables and waiting for the morning session to break, their principal duty was to shoo away the flies that were attracted to the exposed food. This was an especially necessary task because of the four neighboring outhouses in the immediate area and my parents' hog pen located nearby on the backside of the family garden lot. Drinks provided for the delegates consisted of water from the overflow and the tub of lemonade. Although ice tea and coffee were common drinks, I don't recall that either was served at this dinner on the ground. As soon as the session was dismissed for lunch, the delegates poured from the church, gathered around the tables, and, following a short prayer, proceeded to devour the food while continuing to discuss the affairs of the conference. During the course of the meal, my father and I dispensed a lot of lemonade, all the while noting the huge appetites of some delegates who thoroughly enjoyed the wholesome food that the ladies of the church had prepared. A lot of food was consumed that day.

I especially remember this particular dinner on the ground because of a warning that my mother had given me about the food that was likely to appear on the table. When it came to matters in the kitchen, my mother was fastidious about cleanliness. And rightfully so! This was a time when very few of the church members had refrigerators and other means for cooling and preserving food. Furthermore, few of the houses were properly screened and flies moved freely through open windows and doors and were controlled only with fly swatters or sticky traps hanging from the ceiling. In the past she had observed the preparation of food in other members' kitchens and had reached specific conclusions about the level of cleanliness she found there. Consequently, she surveyed the loaded dinner table and instructed me to avoid certain foods that she knew had come from kitchens that did not meet her personal standards of cleanliness. Consequently, my choices from the table were limited to her food and that of a few selected church members, such as my Aunt Marybelle, whose kitchen she judged to be as clean as hers. Of course, this eliminated some fine looking food, especially the pies and cakes. In looking back, I am sure that many of my mother's fears about the cleanliness of food prepared by various ladies of the church were exaggerated or unwarranted. Nevertheless, she was justifiably concerned that we not consume anything that might jeopardize our health. Although an infrequent occurrence, cases of food poisoning in the area did occur (for example, Jesse, the small son of Blaine Hester, an uncle of my mother, died from eating a left-over can of sardines) and this raised her concern about food and its preparation. I don't recall hearing that any of the delegates who dined that day came down with any intestinal or other forms of illnesses as a consequence of eating what the church ladies had prepared. Had there been any kind of outbreak of illnesses following the meal, I am certain the news would have spread rapidly throughout the congregation.

Following the meal, the delegates, many of whom enjoyed the shade of the oaks while eating, reassembled into White Oak Church, leaving various members, mostly women, to do the clean up. Just as rapidly as they had loaded the table, the working ladies removed the remainder of the food, dishes, glasses, and tablecloths. These items disappeared into baskets or sacks and were soon gone from the scene. My father and I had taken time from dispensing lemonade to eat, but in closing out our responsibility, we had another glass of cold lemonade, poured out the rest into the ditch, rinsed out the wash tub at the overflow, and called it a day. Dinner on the ground was over.

Daniel Edmund and Excie Ann Edwards Hester, parents
of the Hester family and leading founders of the White
Oak Original Free Will Baptist Church of Bladenboro,
NC. Credit: Herman Hester

A Sunday congregation at White Oak (circa 1938-1939)
Note large number of young people. The author stands
to the right of the tall girl dressed in white in center of
picture. Credit: Marie Wilson.

Early example of washing the disciples feet.
Credit: F.W.B. Historical Collection, Mount
Olive College, North Carolina

Rev. Walter L. Jernigan, pastor and evangelist who
baptized the author in June Singletary's mill pond.
Credit: F. W. B.
Historical Collection, Mt. Olive College, North Carolina.

Some church leaders. From left to right: Cornelia Gainey, Bliss Hester,
Ada Wilson, Graham Wilson, Hattie Adcox, Willie Bowen,
Carrie E. Suggs, the author's mother.
Credit: Author.

From left to right, sisters Carrie E. Suggs and Marybelle
E. Pait, pianists at White Oak Church. Credit: Author.

The Reverends Herman Wooten (L) and H. C. Adcox (R).

Sterl and Marie Phinney, foreign missionaries, with
their first son. Marie, only child of Graham and Ada
Wilson, was first missionary from White Oak Church.
Credit: Author.

Rev. Milton L. Johnson who tearfully pled with the White
Oak congregation to support the fledgling Mt. Olive College.
Credit: F. W. B. Historical Collection, Mt. Olive College

Rev. Herman Wooten, controversial pastor and builder
of the present White Oak Original Free Will Baptist
Church in Bladenboro. Credit: F. W. B. Historical
Collection, Mt. Olive College.

Original structure of White Oak Original Free Will Baptist
Church, Bladenboro, North Carolina before addition of
classrooms on sides and rear. Credit: Marie W. Phinney.

Church (2009) built during the pastorate of Rev. Herman Wooten
during the nineteen forties. Credit: Author

Excie E. Hester, matriarch of the Hester family, whose
death caused great grief among the members of White
Oak Church. Credit: Herman Hester.

James Fred Davis, son of Roy and Ruby Davis and
close friend of the author. Credit: Frankie Roberts.

W. Graham Wilson, devout member of White Oak
Church whose death was greatly mourned by the
Bladenboro community. Credit: Bladenboro
Historical Museum.

CHAPTER 8

Music in White Oak Church

I will sing unto the Lord as long as I live:
I will sing praise to my God while I have my being.
Psalm 104:33 KJV

For me, the most enjoyable feature of worship at White Oak Church was the music that was an essential part of every religious meeting that I attended there, whether at the regular Sunday services, the revivals, or the Wednesday evening prayer services. While growing up, I had regularly participated in the children's "choir," and I suppose that my involvement there had much to do with my continuing enjoyment of hymns, "special" music, and so on. Although I often resented being called from the congregation with other children to sing, deep down inside I really looked forward to children's choir. Furthermore, my mother was very involved in the music of the church, frequently serving as the church's pianist and with several other ladies, often providing the "special" music in the form of duets and trios. And, both my mother and father also enjoyed singing the old hymns that were part of every service.

We were fortunate to have at home an upright piano that our family had purchased from the Fred Williams family while living on the Old Mill village of the Bladenboro Cotton Mills in the early thirties, and my mother, who later taught piano lessons to neighborhood children, loved to play the instrument at home and sing there the hymns that we sang at church and also songs from the "Yellow Songbook." Occasionally she would play sheet music of popular songs that she had acquired. Once R. J. Hester, her Uncle Bob's oldest son, returned from a stay in New York City and brought back a batch of popular sheet music and asked her to play selected pieces that he liked, for example, "Harbor

Lights." Although not highly sophisticated, music, especially religious music, was very much a part of my life while growing up. I loved to hear my mother play the piano and sing. For possibly these reasons, I found the singing of hymns the most enjoyable part of the religious services at White Oak Church. Even today this remains true for me when attending religious services. I suppose that if I ever get to heaven that it will be on the wings of a song and not through the persuasive words of a preacher.

The music program—if it can be called a program—at White Oak Church centered around the annual election of a pianist who assumed responsibility for playing the piano until re-elected or displaced in the next round of elections. There were three ladies in the church who were sufficiently competent to accompany the congregation in its singing of hymns: Carrie E. Suggs, my mother; Aunt Marybelle Pait, sister to my mother; and Mary Storms. A fourth lady, Hattie Adcox, had a smattering of skill on the piano but was limited by her inability to play any music not in "shaped" notes. Of the three principal musicians, my mother and Aunt Marybelle were the most skilled and capable in playing a greater variety of hymns and accompanying the congregation.

In the absence of a formal program of music, other than occasional solos or duets much of what went on musically was impromptu or without advance preparation. For example, there was no director to lead the choir which, itself, changed from Sunday to Sunday. On Sunday mornings, a few volunteer members of the congregation gathered near the piano at the front of the church where the floor was slightly elevated and where about a dozen straight-backed chairs had been placed in rows. The composition of this group constantly changed around a core of a few steady singers, including David Hester, Graham Wilson, Mary Storms, Marybelle Pait, Cornelia Gainey, Bliss Hester, and my mother. Anyone from the congregation was free to become part of this informal "choir," and it was not unusual for new faces to appear for a Sunday or two and then return to their regular seats. My father and Uncle David J. Pait, my Aunt Marybelle's husband, were among these infrequent volunteers. I don't recall anyone in this make-do choir whose voice reflected unusual talent.

The nearest thing to a choir director at White Oak Church was the Sunday School superintendent whose job it was to emcee the proceedings, especially on those Sundays when there was no "preaching" scheduled.

During my youth in the church, I remember three men who performed this responsibility, although there must have been more. These men were Bliss Hester, David Hester, and Graham Wilson. Generally, prior to the congregation breaking up to enter classes for Bible study, several songs were sung. The superintendents, none of whom had any marked talent for singing, usually requested that someone in the congregation suggest a song, a request that always resulted in a show of several hands. The person at whom the superintendent pointed called out a page number from the hymnal. The pianist then turned to the number to determined whether she was familiar with the song and, if so, when ready she played it accompanied by the congregation. Rarely did anyone select a song that the pianist was unable to play. Before disassembling for classes, several songs were selected and sung. The proceedings were entirely impromptu with nothing planned. When the congregation reassembled after classes, the same song selection procedure was followed with another song or two being sung before the service ended. Through the years, at one time or another the congregation sang most of the songs in the church hymnal, some of them many, many times.

As a boy participating in these services, I absorbed these hymns and they became an essential part of my religious and musical background together with the music taught in the public schools. However, sometimes the most inconsequential part of the musical sessions at church caught my attention. For example, Superintendent David Hester, a rather tall, lanky man, had an extremely prominent Adam's apple and often while singing, I found myself fascinated by the up-and-down movement of this part of his anatomy. And Superintendent Graham Wilson, one of the most respected, devout men I ever knew, always stood with both feet planted together, rocking to-and-fro, while singing in his highly pitched voice and tightly clutching the hymnal with both hands. As I looked at him, the thought often crossed my boyish mind that he was in great danger of tilting either too far forward or backward onto the floor. But led by such men and the pianists, the members of the congregation made a joyful noise in song unto the Lord. My impression was that the members thoroughly enjoyed singing the old hymns of Fanny Crosby, Isaac Watts, Charles Wesley, and many others. I think that the songs momentarily took them away from their present troubles by reminding them that trouble is the universal lot of man.

As Sunday after Sunday passed, I began to identify certain songs with specific individuals in the congregation, so much so that even today when I hear a particular hymn, that person will come to mind. I think that this identification occurred because of the method used in selecting the songs that were sung on Sunday morning. An individual would raise his hand and if recognized would usually request the singing of his favorite hymn whose words and melody had unusual meaning for that person. Occasionally, a member would let it be known that a specific hymn was his favorite. In this manner I gradually came to associate certain songs with different individuals in the church. For example, I never hear "It Is Well With My Soul" without thinking of Graham Wilson. A favorite of Walter Jernigan, a former pastor of White Oak Church, was "Blessed Assurance." When hearing "Work, For The Night Is Coming," I always think of Hattie Adcox because she frequently played the song at prayer meetings. It apparently was the only song she knew how to play on the piano without "shaped" notes. Her husband, H. C. Adcox, a retired minister, loved to sing "What A Friend We Have In Jesus." "Jesus Is All The World To Me" and "It's So Sweet to Trust in Jesus" always reminds me of my mother, and "Blest Be The Tie That Binds" makes me think of my Great Aunt Maryanne Davis. "Where He Leads Me," "Happy Day" and "Higher Ground" were my father's favorites. And there are other hymns that throw me back into time when I was part of the White Oak Church congregation, songs that bring back memories of special music. I always think of my mother and Cornelia Gainey when I hear "His Eye Is On The Sparrow," which they sang several times as a duet.

Perhaps one of the richest legacies of the music at White Oak Church was a discovery I made after leaving the church. As I lived in different parts of the country and attended a variety of denominational, Protestant churches, I found that when the singing began I felt right at home. For rarely did I hear hymns that I had not heard many, many times as a boy while attending White Oak. Whether the Protestant church was Baptist, Methodist, Nazarene, Presbyterian, Church of God, Lutheran, or whatever, I was always familiar with most of the hymns that were sung.

Although without a music program, for me the informal singing of hymns at White Oak Church and the memories associated with them are among the greatest contribution of the church to my spiritual development as a youth. I shall always be grateful for that heritage. In my later years, it has often occurred to me that despite the superficial differences existing among various Protestant denominations, the familiar and common music found in their hymnals has made it possible for me to feel comfortable while worshiping in other churches. The knowledge of the theology found in these hymns, musically expressed, is one of the major links that bind Protestant denominations together. It is a universal link. The denominations may differ in how they interpret Scriptural phrases and how they practice their rituals, but their musical heritage—at least, up until the recent upsurge in contemporary services with their repetitive, noisy use of choruses accompanied by amplified musical instruments—is a common bond that helps to make them more alike than different.

CHAPTER 9

Church Democracy

For it hath been declared unto me of you, my brethren,
by them which are of the house of Chloe, that there are
contentions among you. Now this
I say, that everyone of you saith, I am of Paul; and
I of Appollos; and I of Cephas; and I of Christ.
1 Corinthians 1: 11-12 KJV

For anyone to think that peace, love and harmony always characterize the relationship of professing "born again" Christians within church congregations reveals conclusively that he has never been a long-time member of any religious body. It is true that ideally the human tendency to be disagreeable toward one's fellow man or one's fellow Christians should never find expression within a sanctuary dedicated to furthering the gospel message of Christ. However, as much as one would like to think otherwise, some congregations are periodically marked by as much wrangling among the membership over issues—sometime very trivial issues—as in any other social institution. Human foibles and disagreements over outside secular matters are frequently and unintentionally brought into the worship service and the affairs of the church, affecting and overcoming in a negative way the whole purpose of its being. When this occurs, it seems that the Gospel is overcome by the world rather than the world being overcome by the Gospel.

White Oak Church was not immune to these sporadic spats among its members, some involving serious issues and others involving trivial issues. One of the more serious issues that involved the maintenance of authentic financial records during the construction of a new sanctuary has been alluded to in another place in this work. There were others that seemed to be generated out of a deliberate desire to inject—seemingly for the fun of it—mayhem into normal church proceedings. These usually occurred during sessions when leadership positions in the church were being determined by elections.

As a member of the Free Will Baptist denomination, White Oak Church enjoyed complete congregational autonomy in the selection of its pastors and other leaders. Every year electoral decisions were made concerning leadership positions, for example, the selection of Sunday School superintendent, teachers for the various classes, pianist, church treasurer, and so on. Most of these positions went to volunteers who were known to be very willing to spend the time and effort to carry out the responsibilities of office. Consequently, at the time of annual elections the congregation usually had no difficulty in easily filling some positions that were necessary for the church to function. But, as I recall, there were two jobs in the church that often led to "hurt feelings" among members of the congregation. One involved the selection of the pianist for the coming year; the other concerned either the retention or the selection of a new pastor if, for some reason, there was a vacancy.

The fuss over the selection of the pianist was one of the trivial spats provoked by certain elements of the Hester family who made up the majority of church members. Some of the younger Hesters were a devilish group who, as my Great-Grandma Excie Hester would have said, had a "touch of the Ole Nick" that came into play when the congregation was selecting the pianist. There were two sisters in the church, granddaughters of Excie, who were equally skilled at playing the piano and accompanying the congregation in the singing of hymns—my Aunt Marybelle Pait and my mother, Carrie Suggs. When it came time to select the pianist, inevitably one of the two would be nominated to be the church musician for the coming year, and just as inevitably, one of the younger Hesters would nominate the other sister, thereby creating a contest between the two siblings who were already naturally competitive. The second nomination was usually made with considerable fanfare of utmost seriousness, the intent and purpose of which, however, was to force the congregation to choose between the two sisters in an effort to create dismay and disharmony between them.

The perpetrators were usually successful, because each sister loved to play the piano for the congregation. The nominations prompted the siblings to rise simultaneously and graciously vie with each other in declining the nomination, much to the delight of some elements of the congregation. The sisters' attempt to defer to each other produced what seemed to some church members to be a minor family squabble, exactly what the nominators had intended. With knowing looks, winks and snickers, they and their supporters sat back and enjoyed watching the sisters squirm as each sought to insist that the other should have the position. As a result, whatever the outcome of the election, regardless of which sister won, the other was invariably left uncomfortable and disappointed at her failure to have a majority of the congregation, which included close relatives like aunts and uncles, select her as pianist for the coming year. It was a near certainty that the following year the same kind of contest over the position of church pianist would again ensue to the discomfort of the two sisters.

Although the annual election of the church pianist provided an opportunity for a few devilish members of the church to have a little fun at the expense of two sisters equally skilled at the piano, the episode amounted to very little in the on-going practices of the church. For example, in the absence of the elected pianist, the other sister, if present, graciously accompanied the congregation in the singing of hymns. In contrast, however, at times the election of a minister for the coming year produced a serious brouhaha that caused some members to seriously consider renouncing their membership and moving on to another Free Will Baptist church, perhaps even to a different denomination.

There were often extraneous contributing factors that made these occasional pastoral elections so passionate and upsetting to some members, factors that had nothing to do with the qualifications of the minister involved. As mentioned above, the descendants of Daniel and Excie Hester composed the majority of the congregation, and their son Bob was the obvious leader of this group. Ill feelings among the Hester relatives or persons incorporated into the family by marriage was an element sometimes factored into the selection of the minister. Or, fundamental differences and disagreements among members of the congregation—not necessarily just the Hesters—involving church plans and activities also found expression when choosing the minister, for hostile feelings silently at work in the congregation sometimes surfaced and played a role in determining the outcome. And, occasionally, in trying to be helpful a member might unintentionally antagonize another. For example, I recall that once there was a serious falling out between two members because one, seeking to be helpful in a spirit of love, informed the other that her teenage daughter had been seen in the company of a married man. It took awhile for good feelings to be restored between the two ladies who were related to each other.

Sometimes the fear by certain older leaders that their positions of influence were being challenged by younger church members came into play. Once during the course of an election, as a teenager I made the unfortunate mistake of pointing out to the "moderator" conducting an election (Rev. H. C. Adcox, a superannuated minister) that his procedures were violating Roberts Rules of Order. Much to my surprise the reverend told me to sit down and be quiet, a command that humiliated me but which I instantly obeyed. It was abundantly clear that he wanted no interference, especially by a youth, in his conduct of the election. Of course, my chastisement in front of the congregation by this elderly, retired minister also greatly upset my parents. This personal putdown demonstrated that the election of a pastor for White Oak Church could conceivably involve factors other than the qualifications of the minister himself.

A prime example of discord when electing a minister occurred during the late forties when the congregation had to decide whether to return the Rev. Herman Wooten for another year or elect someone else to replace him as pastor. At the time, White Oak Church was deeply involved in building a new sanctuary. Logically, therefore, the re-election of the preacher-contractor overseeing the work should have been a non-event. But, as alluded to elsewhere, Rev. Wooten was first and foremost a builder who sometimes allowed his drive to construct as many church buildings as possible to overshadow and interfere with his responsibility as a minister of the Gospel. There were times when his market values conflicted with his Christian values. In his capacity as a building contractor responsible for constructing the new White Oak Church, there were moments when he seemed to forget his role as builder of the intangible church that the new, modern facility would house.

It was the reverend's tendency to forget his calling as a minister of the Gospel that led to his alienation from my father and a few others and precipitated one of the memorable elections that I observed while a youthful member of the congregation. Because he was recognized by the church community and the members of the building committee as a dependable, honest man whose word was his bond, my father was chosen treasurer for the building project. From the start he was determined to faithfully record every penny raised and spent on the new sanctuary. However from the initiation of construction, he found that his decision to maintain complete and accurate records of expenditures would be difficult.

Immediately requests came from the pastor for funds to pay bills for construction materials that had not been submitted to the treasurer, coupled with refusals by the preacher to provide personal receipts when his requests for funds were granted. There were also disagreements between the two about promises that had been made to Raymond Gainey, Cornelia Gainey's son, concerning the per hour wage to be paid for his labor on the new church. As mentioned elsewhere, the Gaineys had agreed to demolish the old church and part of the arrangement was that Raymond was to have a job helping to construct the new church with a per hour wage of seventy-five cents. Rev. Wooten attempted to renege on this promise, and was joined by two other members of the building committee—Rev. Adcox and Bob Hester—in insisting that Raymond be paid less than promised. While treasurer, my father refused to reduce Raymond's pay. He became even more disenchanted with the preacher when he suggested that a key of nails inadvertently not itemized on a bill from Hussey's Builders Supply not be paid. My father refused the suggestion and paid for the nails. As a result, his confidence in the spiritual quality of the preacher and his supporters soured. Such episodes caused a struggle to ensue between the two opposing factions over the legitimate use of funds and maintenance of proper records. Because they were strong supporters of Rev. Wooten, Bob Hester and Rev. Adcox were inclined to overlook his flaws.

An important extraneous factor entered into the growing disagreement. In the Old Mill where my father was once employed, for many years Bob Hester had been a supervisor with power to hire and fire. His position, therefore, gave him considerable influence both in the workplace and in the White Oak Church congregation that was principally composed of relatives and other mill families. Several years after his marriage to my mother, Hester's niece, my father had a major disagreement with Hester in the Old Mill over his promise to award a choice work assignment of running a set of frames. Instead, contrary to his promise Hester gave the job to another worker and attempted to assign my father to the job of "sweeper," the dirtiest job in the mill. The job involved chipping away congealed snuff and tobacco spit that had accumulated around the support beams of the mill. Not a tobacco user, he refused the job. Hester's broken promise and my father's refusal to work as a sweeper led to an argument between the two, leading Hester angrily to demand that he take the sweeping job or be fired. Rather than do so, he quit, left town, and sought employment in a cotton mill in St. Pauls. That he quit and left his family to search for work during the Great Depression when jobs were limited is a measure of how intensely my father felt about his mistreatment. However, he was soon back in town, and by action of a sympathetic general superintendent of the Bladenboro Cotton Mills, he began work in its New Mill operating frames like the ones he had been promised by Hester. His employment there placed him beyond Hester's reach.

The disagreement in the workplace of the Old Mill left Hester and my father with enduring ill feelings toward each other that their membership in White Oak Church never overcame. Rarely did my father dislike anyone, but I don't think that he ever had much respect for Bob Hester after the broken promise and the argument in the Old Mill. Years later this mutual dislike, I am sure, most likely strengthened Hester's support of Rev. Wooten in his conflict with my father. The workplace disagreement between these two members of the congregation is an example of how extraneous matters sometimes created inter-congregational tensions that often affect the outcome of elections for church leaders and other issues.

As the patriarch of the large extended family of Hesters that composed the majority membership in White Oak Church, Bob Hester successfully influenced nearly all of them to follow his leadership on most of the issues that came before the church for decision. In the election to determine whether Herman Wooten would remain minister for another year, Hester and Rev. Adcox of the building committee strongly supported Wooten. Hester rallied most of his relatives to fall in line and vote as he did, this despite their awareness that at times the minister's actions were known to be incompatible with the Christian doctrine he preached. With their support, Rev. Wooten easily carried the election, winning out, as I recall, over a highly-thought-of former pastor who was favored by a minority of members. The outcome caused my father to resign immediately as treasurer of the building committee.

The committee then elected an unenthusiastic but compliant Warren Hester, another of Bob's nephews, from whom no opposition to the preacher's antics was expected. Unhappy over his inability to carry out the duties of treasurer in the proper manner, and generally unhappy with the quality of church leadership, my father gradually lost interest in the activities at White Oak Church and eventually transferred his membership to the First Baptist Church of Bladenboro where he and my mother, who also became disenchanted with the church, were contented and happy members for decades before their deaths.

Although occasional conflict was evident in the life of White Oak Church, I don't think that it was the dominant characteristic. There were enough devout members whose influence was pervasive enough to keep these sporadic surface eruptions from getting completely out of hand and destroying the church. Furthermore, there were too many family ties, too many common life experiences, and too many associations in the workplace for these "fallings out" to have a lasting effect on the majority of the members. Nevertheless, at times dissensions did occur with the result some members left the church and sought spiritual sustenance elsewhere. They simply packed their spiritual bags and moved on. Yet, today, the "new" church built with so much unhappiness for some members during the pastorship of Rev. Wooten still stands and thrives, which is a tribute to the spiritual resiliency of the changing congregation.

CHAPTER 10

Visitors to White Oak Church

All hail the power of Jesus' name,
Let angels prostrate fall.
Bring forth the royal diadem,
And crown Him Lord of All.

Edward Perronet & Oliver Holden

While a member of White Oak Church, I don't recall many non-members, distinguished or otherwise, who visited the congregation. The years of the Great Depression and World War II were hard years for everyone, kind of stay-at-home years for small town residents, and there was not much about the church and its activities that would attract anyone other than its regular members to attend services there. A possible exception were times of revivals that frequently enticed visitors—usually members from nearby local churches—to visit, especially if word spread in the community that there was a "lot of good preaching" by an out-of-town preacher and a "lot of good singing" going on. Otherwise, changes in the congregation resulted from youngsters joining the church or older members dying. Year after year faces remained essentially the same with slight, indiscernible changes with the passage of time. An influx of visitors was not a hallmark of White Oak Church. Nevertheless, I do remember three occasions when visitors came that might be described as memorable in that they made a very great impression on me.

Graham and Ada Wilson were very important members of our congregation, not only because of their regular attendance and financial support but also because they were an extremely devout couple whose lives reflected their faith and beliefs. As noted elsewhere, most members of White Oak Church worked in the Bladenboro Cotton Mills, making it essentially a working-class church. In contrast, Mr Graham—he was always called that—worked as the lead clerk in the dry goods department of the Bridger Corporation, the leading mercantile establishment in Bladenboro. Mrs. Ada—everyone called her that—was a frail-looking housewife. Each of them was highly influential in all the activities of White Oak Church. I remember the public prayers of Mrs. Ada, which helped to build my vocabulary. (Mrs. Ada once used the terms "finite" and "infinite" in a prayer that sent me afterwards to the home dictionary to explore their meanings.) And I remember the ever-ready willingness of Mr. Graham to help members of the congregation. As one of the few members of the congregation with a car, he was frequently called upon to drive sick members to out-of-town hospitals. For example, as a boy I recall a cold, starry night riding with my father in the rumble seat of Mr. Graham's Model A Ford as we returned with my mother after her visit to the clinic at Duke University Hospital in Durham. Furthermore, I also recall the spiritual interest both of them took in me as a boy: Mrs. Ada, fearful of what she called the evils of "modernism," encouraged me to become a minister and go to a Bible college rather than Wake Forest College where terrible things like "evolution" were said to be taught, and Mr. Graham took me on fishing trips to June Singletary's and Fred Nance's millponds when stores in town shut down on Wednesday afternoon for a mid-week break. Upon his death from cancer of the esophagus around 1945, nearly all the stores in Bladenboro shut down for his funeral and burial at Oak Grove Free Will Baptist Church off the Dublin road. The Wilsons were a wonderful, devout couple who had only one child, Marie.

At an early age, Marie concluded that God had "called" her to spend her life in foreign missions. Devout Christians themselves, the Wilsons respected their daughter's decision and sent her out of state to Marion College in Indiana (now Indiana Wesleyan University), at that time a far distant place from the little village of Bladenboro, to prepare for her life's work as a Christian missionary abroad. While at college, the inevitable happened. Although she had left behind a young man named LeRoy Brown, who dearly loved her, at college she met Sterl Phinney, a young man who, too, had felt the call to serve in foreign missions. They fell in love and were married. My mother, who was a contemporary and good friend of Marie, often spoke of the sacrifice that the Wilsons had made in allowing their only child to leave home for a far away college, and then having her return married to someone destined to take her even farther away into distant countries. I think that the Wilsons simply accepted these separations as sacrifices in conformity to the will of God for their daughter. With her husband, Marie spent years serving in Latin American countries and in Japan shortly before the outbreak of World War II. With war clouds threatening between Japan and the United States, the Phinney family returned home, and it was on their temporary return to Bladenboro that White Oak Church hosted what I now remember as truly memorable visitors.

In honor of the occasion, the church arranged for a special Sunday evening service where Marie and her family were to talk about their experiences as missionaries and to show selected memorabilia from their travels. The meeting was the church's way of honoring not only the outstanding religious work of one of its own, but also to honor Mrs. Ada and Mr. Graham who had spent years separated from their daughter, her husband and their grandchildren. As I recall the Phinneys had two or three boys who accompanied them to the evening service. The program called for both the Phinneys to speak, Sterl to deliver a sermon and Marie to speak generally about their lives abroad and to show a few items they had collected.

One reason these visitors made such an impression on me was that the Wilsons were such good friends of our family, my mother was a friend of Marie, and the way the service began. It started with a hymn that was not part of the usual White Oak Church repertoire, and was led rather enthusiastically by Sterl. At the church piano was my mother, as noted above, a good friend of Marie and one of several women who provided music for the congregation. The song was "All Hail the Power of Jesus' Name" which, after the first verse or two, the congregation joined in singing loudly. I don't remember anything at all about the sermon that evening (it must have been on the subject of missions) and very little about anything said by Marie in describing their experiences as missionaries. I only have vivid memories of their faces that night and their choice of that first song. To this day, every time I hear "All Hail the Power of Jesus' Name" sang in church, my mind moves quickly back to the evening at White Oak when one of its most cherished daughters, one who had forsaken father, mother and a young man who loved her, in order to spread the Word in foreign mission fields, returned home briefly to Bladenboro to tell us, as she put it, about her work for the Lord.

Another memorable visit to White Oak was that of a group of youngsters from an orphanage that the Free Will Baptist denomination maintained at Middlesex, North Carolina. Ten to twelve orphans with their leaders arrived on a Sunday to present a musical program that evening for the congregation. The purpose of the visit was to generate support for the orphanage and its children. The young people were dispersed among nearby members of the church who had agreed to feed and house them overnight. This was the same arrangement used for taking care of the bi-monthly visits of its preachers because the church could afford neither a permanent pastor nor a parsonage.

I suppose that the visit of this group from the orphanage made such a lasting, personal impression was because prior to its visit, my father and I, together with perhaps a half-dozen members of the congregation, had visited the orphanage at Middlesex in a trip that remains unforgettable because of the way we traveled. I don't recall the purpose of our visit, but it was probably to demonstrate the interest of the church in supporting the institution. At the time there was very little public support available for widows or orphans, except the poor farm. There was no social networks then as there is now to help unfortunate people whose lives had been thrown into disarray by hard luck, that is, individuals who had fallen through the "cracks." And, with times so hard in the depression years, there was practically no great amount of aid forthcoming from churches like White Oak. My father may have had a more personal reason for volunteering for the trip. As noted elsewhere, my mother had a heart condition that occasionally frightened her into thinking that she was near death, and at such times she had expressed her wish that should that occur, she wanted her boys (my brother Charles and me) placed in the orphanage at Middlesex. Under no circumstances would my father have fulfilled that wish and separated himself from his sons, but he may have taken the trip to please her.

Few members of White Oak then owned cars, certainly no one possessed a vehicle that could transport the half-dozen or more people who volunteered for the Middlesex visit. Consequently, to make the trip someone proposed that the church hire a flat-bed truck and driver from Cary Dowless or Grover Pait, who owned small trucking firms in Bladenboro, and that is how we traveled to Middlesex—riding openly on a flat bed truck. I recall that I was just a boy when this great adventure occurred. With other men, Dad and I sat precariously on the bouncing bed of the truck as we sped to Middlesex. (It was my second experience in riding dangerously and uneasily on a flat bed with my father holding me tightly. Earlier, we had traveled in like manner with mill worker friends to Tully Singletary's burial at Butters located several miles from Bladenboro.) We arrived safely at the orphanage in time to have lunch in a small dining hall with a lot of youngsters—many of whom were approximately my age—and their supervisors, and then after a short, guided tour of the facility we placed ourselves on the flat bed and returned safely home. On the return trip we passed through St. Pauls. I shall never forget the look of disbelief on the faces of bystanders as we rumbled nosily through the town, my father desperately clinging to me during that wild ride.

The program presented by the chorus from the orphanage at Middlesex was one of sacred music. As I sat and listened to the children sing that evening, I was very much aware of my mother's recurring "spells" with her heart that might cause her death. I couldn't help but think that except for a loving father, my brother and I might some day join them at the orphanage in Middlesex. The performers were a nice looking group of young people, they sang very well, and the congregation was delighted to hear them. Of the hymns that they sang that evening, I only remember one—"Fairest Lord Jesus." Whenever I hear this hymn, I am thrown back into time, and I see once again that small group of orphans standing in front of the congregation singing their hearts out. And I remember, too, that crazy trip with my father and a few other male members of the congregation riding through St. Pauls with all those unbelieving bystanders staring as we passed. Following the program, there was a "free will" offering or "collection" taken in behalf of the children. After spending the night with church members, the orphans went on their way to perform at another church.

While attending White Oak Church as a boy, there was a commonly held belief among substantial numbers of Free Will Baptists that a divine "call" to preach was all that was necessary for one to enter the ministry. This view was not restricted solely to the Free Will Baptist denomination. For example, a number of men in local evangelical churches—men such as Gaston Hester, Luther Smith, Holland Hughes and others who worked in the Bladenboro Cotton Mills—received the "call" and launched careers in the ministry while maintaining their jobs in the mills. These working-class preachers and the churches that licensed them to preach truly believed that the absence of any formal, educational preparation for the ministry was not an obstacle to their expounding the intricacies of the Bible. Some were successful, working full time and preaching part-time until they could move into full-time preaching. Like the members of the congregations from which they emerged, they believed that God having called them to preach removed the necessity to expand their knowledge of anything but the Bible, and that whatever enlightenment they needed would come directly from above. God would provide all the help and inspiration needed to fulfill a successful ministry, and God would lay his message on their hearts and empower them to preach the Word, unafraid, as he wanted it preached. It being God's will—as evidenced by his "call" that they should preach—they felt assured that with God supporting their effort whatever they possessed intellectually was enough. Education was not a high priority for believers who accepted this view of the ministry.

Although this view of the ministry was certainly widespread among the members of White Oak Church, there were some indications that a slow but discernible change was in progress. For example, upon learning of their daughter Marie's desire to serve the Lord as a missionary, Graham and Ada Wilson sacrificially allowed her to enroll in a college far from home in order that she might be better prepared for what lay ahead. And there were other indications of a turning from the old view that "what you have is enough" among certain leaders of the Free Will Baptists in eastern North Carolina who had concluded that the salvation of the denomination lay in making possible higher, Christian education for its young people. For example, a fund was established from which small loans were made available at low interest for college students in the nineteen forties. I was a recipient of such a loan that helped me through my second year at Wake Forest College (now University). And there were denominational leaders who had a greater vision, individuals who thought that their denomination should have its own college, much like the Southern Baptists and the Presbyterians in the area. Such a man was Rev. Milton L. Johnson, Business Manager of the fledgling Mt. Olive College, who, if I remember correctly, once had provided the bi-monthly preaching services at White Oak Church. His return to the church to seek its support for the college was a memorable occasion for me.

While a few individual members in White Oak Church—such as the Wilsons—were aware of how significant were an educated ministry and congregation if the denomination was to survive and flourish, unfortunately it seemed the vast majority of its members thought in opposite terms. Most of these members lacked even a high school education, and it was difficult for them to see the necessity of educating young people who seemed destined to work in either the cotton mills or on nearby farms. And, as indicated above, they believed that if God called a man to preach—it was always a man, never a woman—then God would put the words into his heart and mind to deliver when called upon to do so. Thus there was no reason to waste good money on educating a preacher when God would provide all that he needed. Furthermore, many of them reasoned that they had gotten by without an education, so why should their children spend all that time in school, especially a college, when after reaching the age for a work permit, they could be doing something useful like earning wages in the mills or on the farms. For many members, the upper educational ambition for their children was completion of the eighth grade or high school. So, when Rev. Johnson went to White Oak Church to persuade its members to support the denominational college, he had his work cut out for him.

I have very little recollection about the details and arguments that Johnson used in trying to convince the members of White Oak that they should support the creation of a college for the young Free Will Baptists growing up in the region. I do remember questions from his listeners, some of whom were clearly in opposition to the vision for the denomination that he was presenting. The opposition, as I recall, came principally from some of the lesser educated elements of the congregation who made up the bulk of both the leadership and membership of the church. Nevertheless, there were a few members (for example, my mother) who voiced support for sustaining the college, and, of course, the Wilsons supported the idea. And, there were a few others, such as my Aunt Marybelle. But what I remember most about Johnson's visit was the passion he showed while making his case for the college. That is what lingers in my mind. During his presentation, there were times when it seemed to me that he was near tears when, perhaps, he realized that his arguments were falling on many deaf ears. At the end of the session, the matter was left in limbo. However, Johnson did leave with the knowledge that within the congregation, there were a few members whom he had enlightened and whom he could count on to do what they could to fulfill his dream and that of others. In fairness to those who opposed a commitment of financial support, the times were such that many of the members had difficulty supporting themselves.

Fortunately, the less enlightened among the Free Will Baptists in eastern North Carolina did not thwart the vision of Johnson and other leaders that the future of the denomination lay with an educated ministry and a membership whose children would have access to higher education at an institution imbued with the religious tenets of the denomination. The dream of Johnson and others eventually materialized in what is today Mount Olive College, a thriving liberal arts institution where Free Will Baptists, if they so desire, can send their children knowing that they will continue to be influenced by the beliefs of their denomination.

I am certain that there must have been other visitors, notable or otherwise, who graced the doors of White Oak Church while I was a member there. However, these are the ones that impressed me enough to remember.

CHAPTER 11

Tearing Down the Old Church: Building the New

For we know that if our earthly house of this tabernacle
were dissolved, we have a building of God, an house not
made with hands, eternal in the heavens.
2 Corinthians 5:1

Sometime during the late forties, under the leadership of a newly elected Rev. Herman Wooten the congregation of White Oak Church decided that the time had come to build a new house of worship. I am not certain how the membership arrived at this decision, but I suspect that the recently installed Rev. Wooten had much to do with convincing leading church members that the old sanctuary had become inadequate for the needs of the day. I don't remember ever hearing my parents discuss how the decision was arrived at, especially what the compelling reasons were for launching the construction of a new building.

One thing I did know. The resources of the congregation were then so skimpy that the very idea of starting a building program in the immediate aftermath of World War II seemed ludicrous to some members because they feared a return of the Great Depression as industry converted from wartime to peacetime production. It was a period of general uncertainty as the economy shakily readjusted to peace. Furthermore, the parishioners were not wealthy. Most of them lived from one payday to the next with no savings in reserve. I remember once when the old church needed a new roof, it was necessary for some of its members, including my father, to visit and request a donation for that purpose from the president of the Bladenboro Cotton Mills. Without his generosity, there would have been no new roof, for the church alone could not then afford it. Nevertheless, Rev. Wooten, who had a history of building churches, together with church leaders, successfully persuaded the congregation that a new building was needed and that the financial risks were manageable despite the scarcity of resources.

After the decision had been made to replace the old sanctuary, a building committee was set up to direct the construction of the new. Its members consisted of about a half-dozen of the most active individuals of the congregation. My father agreed to be the treasurer of the enterprise, a position that later he very much regretted having assumed. It was his responsibility to collect and disburse the money collected through donations and loans as the project progressed. Other members included the Rev. Wooten, the Rev. Adcox, Willie Bowens, Bob Hester, Graham Wilson and there may have been others whom I don't remember. It was the responsibility of this committee to oversee and make all decisions concerning the construction of the new sanctuary. As I recall from conversations with my father, the decision-making process within the committee quickly fell under control of Rev. Wooten, Rev. Adcox, and Hester. Of these three, Rev. Wooten had a direct, perhaps conflicting, interest in building the new church. Although the church's minister, he was selected to supervise its construction for which he would be paid a salary in addition to that that he received as minister.

One of the earliest problems confronting the committee was to decide where to locate the new structure. The old building set well back on church property almost to the south property line, thereby eliminating the possibility that the new church could be located behind the old. My parents' property abutted the church's property to the east, and Rev. Adcox's property joined the church's property to the west. Consequently, unless the new church was to move to an entirely new location, it was necessary to build it in front of the old sanctuary, placing it on what had been the parking lot of the old. However, in doing so, the front of the new structure would be situated unusually close to Highway 211 with very limited parking, except along the side of the highway, and its rear would be unusually close to the old building. Nevertheless, rather than build the church on an entirely new site, the committee decided to locate the new church in the parking lot. (The resulting parking problem was partially solved by the removal of the old church and, years later, by the acquisition of the Adcox, Suggs, Talley Kinlaw,and Joe Stubbs properties adjacent to the church) Probably because of the expense and the inconvenience to core families who lived near the existing church, I don't think that the committee ever gave any serious consideration to relocating at a new site.

Of course, financing the new construction presented a problem for a congregation not burdened with wealth. A teenager at the time, I was neither interested in nor did I become acquainted with the committee's decisions regarding the method of funding the building of a more modern sanctuary. Although my father was for a time the treasurer of the enterprise, I remember very little family discussion about how construction was to be financed. Typically, however, the Bladenboro Cotton Mills would be asked to make a donation because the bulk of White Oak's membership consisted of mill operatives. However, it was one thing for mill management to make a relatively small donation for replacing a shingled, church roof, and quite another to make a substantial donation to help defray the cost of major construction. It is likely, therefore, that the underwriting for the new building was in the form of loans, possibly from the Bank of Bladenboro or other banks, and sources set aside for new church construction within the Free Will Baptist denomination. And, too, though their means were indeed limited, individual members of the congregation—as well as persons outside the church—may have made contributions to the building fund. And I recall that after the church had been built, the ladies held dinners and suppers in the church basement to raise money to help retire the debt.

Another decision that the building committee had to make was what to do with the old church that had served the congregation so well. Although there was much valuable material in the structure (for example, the sills, rafters and studs were made of heart lumber provided by my maternal grandfather, Charley Edwards), there was no market for used lumber in the small town of Bladenboro where the limited construction then in progress drew building needs exclusively from a newly established building supply outlet owned by Bill and Charles Hussy, who also owned a downtown grocery store. The absence of potential buyers for the church complicated the committee's work. Contracting to have the old church torn down and the debris removed was expensive and an additional burden on the financially strapped congregation. Yet, the empty sanctuary had to be removed because its proximity to the new church would represent a fire hazard. It was at this point that Cornelia Gainey, widowed, longtime church member, and her son, Raymond, who was nearing high school graduation, stepped in and provided a solution. I am not familiar with the precise details of the agreement worked out between the building committee and the Gainey family, but it is my understanding that the Gaineys assumed responsibility for the removal of the old church in return for whatever material that they could salvage. Furthermore, Raymond was to be given a job in construction of the new church, his pay to be seventy-five cents an hour. If there was any other compensation paid to the church, I am not aware of it. With the used lumber, the Gaineys planned to build a small house in nearby Lumberton.

It is at this juncture that I became involved, in a very minor way, in tearing down the old church building. Raymond was then in his late teens, just having graduated from high school, and, needless to say, for him to dismantle White Oak Church was a herculean task. How he and his mother expected him to do so still amazes me. He simply could not tear down that building alone. For awhile during the summer before my senior year in high school, I was available and Raymond and his mother hired me to help with some of the initial stages of the salvage.

With only crowbars and claw hammers, we began our work by dismantling one of the Sunday School classrooms that formed the east and west wings of the church. As noted elsewhere, these annexes had been added some years after the building of the original sanctuary. Unlike today when the studs and rafters of interior walls and ceilings can be quickly covered in sheet rock or paneling, the studs in the classrooms had been laboriously sealed using tongue and grooved pine lumber, narrow in width, nailed directly to the studs with cut nails. The same was true of the ceiling.

Because the Gaineys purpose in dismantling the old church was to salvage as much of its material as possible for use elsewhere, Raymond and I proceeded carefully, experimenting in ways to minimize the damage to each piece of the lumber as we removed it. We quickly discovered that to do so was time consuming, and that with our limited tools it was nearly impossible to remove a single piece without doing some damage to it. Nevertheless, during the summer the piles of salvageable material gradually accumulated as we worked our way slowly through classrooms of the old church. From time to time, Raymond would hire someone to remove the piles from the site and re-stack it near his nearby home on Highway 211.

When school began, it was necessary for me to stop working on the old church. As I recall, other than my work inside the Sunday School classrooms, there was only one other occasion when I assisted Raymond in tearing down the building. When the time came to begin removing the roof and although reluctant to do so because of the height of the church, I agreed to help him strip off the shingles. Thereafter, I had nothing to do with the work. Nevertheless, with other helpers, the building continued to come down bit by bit, including the removal of the church bell that had been located over the front entrance. For some years thereafter, the bell was stored in the Gainey's garage. My last contact with any of the material derived from the old church occurred the next summer when the Gaineys hired me to assist Raymond as he constructed a house in Lumberton. Today, somewhere in Lumberton, remnants of the old White Oak Church is there incorporated in someone's residence.

Tearing down the old church and building a new one was not without its tensions, and these created unhappiness among some members, one of whom was my father who had been asked to serve as treasurer of the building committee. As treasurer he was responsible for handling the finances involved in constructing the new sanctuary. Early on into the project—as mentioned elsewhere—my father became aware that Rev. Wooten, who was both the church's minister and contractor for the new building, was not very interested in maintaining complete and accurate financial records of the many transactions that occurred as construction progressed. In contrast, my father felt exactly the opposite, because he realized that the congregation would hold him completely responsible for how the church's financial resources were used. As a result, a conflict developed within the building committee over this issue and the amount of wages to be paid Raymond Gainey for his work that spilled over into church proceedings, causing the Hester faction and its supporters that had been responsible for Wooten's call as minister to White Oak Church, to rally behind the preacher. Consequently, rather than continue in a position that might later open him up to charges of wrong doing because of incomplete and poorly kept financial records, my father resigned as treasurer and, subsequently, withdrew from the church. He and my mother soon afterwards joined the First Baptist

Church of Bladenboro where they happily remained members until their deaths.

A far more tragic event than my family's unhappiness occurred during the construction of the lower level of the new sanctuary. It was the habit of workers during lunch breaks to cross Highway 211, visit Bill and Mollie Cain's small store, purchase bottled soft drinks, and then return with the refreshments to the construction site to eat and rest. Rarely did they return the empty bottles to the store. Consequently, Bill often sent Larry, his small son, and my brother Charles, then about ten years old, to retrieve these bottles. Once, unfortunately, at the end of the day a worker left his empty bottle on a wall where two joined, unsecured pieces of heavy, two-by-ten lumber had been inserted above an open window space. Later when Larry, who was several years younger than my brother, attempted to reach the empty bottle by climbing into the window space and then trying to pull himself up further using the unsecured lumber to do so, he fell, pulling the heavy beam down upon his head. Although rushed to the hospital in Lumberton, the accident proved fatal. Because of someone's careless failure to secure the beam over the window, the price of a young life was added to the total cost of the new sanctuary.

My last remembered activity for White Oak Church occurred shortly after its completion. Through Rev. Wooten, the church had purchased pews from a construction company located near Raleigh. For some reason Mack Duvall, a former high-school classmate and friend who was not a member of the congregation, was hired to transport the pews from the manufacturer to the church. Mack asked me to help him with the task. With the permission of the father of another mutual friend, Ted Shaw, Mack obtained the use of a flat bed truck with sides. Mack had no chauffeur's license and, as far as I know, had never before driven a large truck, loaded or unloaded, but despite my reluctance to do so, off we went to pick up a large load of pews.

It was a trip of more than a hundred miles! Today's modern highways into Raleigh are not anything like the narrow, dangerous roads that once led into this bustling city during the forties. As I recall that trip, I am amazed that the church building committee hired a late teenager like Mack for such a task, someone who had no experience driving a large truck. I don't believe that anyone on the committee considered the inherent dangers of the trip for a teenage driver, or the matter of church liability had a disastrous wreck with injuries occurred. Furthermore, I am amazed that Ted's father permitted an inexperienced driver the use of his truck, and I am also amazed that my parents, even though they were then church members, allowed their son to help in transporting the pews from Raleigh. Upon arrival at the manufacturers, we loaded approximately fifteen of the long, heavy pews on to the flat bed and somehow safely returned to Bladenboro where we unloaded them at the church. I suspect that there was at least one subsequent load of pews following this first load, but, if so, I had nothing to do with this later trip. As far as I know, the pews that Mack and I delivered to White Oak Church are still in use.

CHAPTER 12

Christmas at White Oak

And there were in the same country shepherds abiding in
the field, keeping watch over their flock by night.
And, lo, the angel of the Lord came upon them, and the
glory of the Lord shone round about them: and they were
sore afraid. Luke 2: 8-9 KJV

Of all the events that occurred at White Oak, Christmas was by far the happiest, especially for the children who every year looked forward to its coming with great anticipation. Like a heavy cloud the Great Depression dominated the thirties, and World War II dominated the early forties, making these two decades extremely difficult for all members of the congregation. Years of economic hardships were followed by years of war, and no church family entirely escaped the hurts brewed by these terrible calamities. Although the church provided an emotional haven from much of the distress produced by depression and war, it was the advent of the Christmas season that provided a welcome distraction, a hopeful respite, from the weighty cares and anxieties of the era. Christmas was a very special time in the lives of church members.

The celebration of Christmas required several weeks of preparation. Although there was no official in the church responsible for appointing a program committee, miraculously such a committee always emerged at Christmas. Year after year it usually consisted of the same half-dozen dozen or so ladies who met informally and decided on which children would do what both to entertain and to cause the congregation to think more deeply about the meaning of Christmas. Among these women were my mother Carrie, my Aunt Marybelle Pait, Hattie Adcox, Mary Storms, Cornelia Gainey, and others whose names I now don't recall.

That these women should be always involved in fashioning the Christmas programs is not surprising, because they were involved as leaders in all activities within the church. At the time all of them were relatively young mothers with children who they naturally wanted involved in any religious activity appropriate for youth. Furthermore, the Christmas program provided an opportunity for children from the nearby mill villages—and there were many children of cotton mill workers in our congregation—to display their talents before the assembled congregation. This was a good thing because, unfortunately, children of mill hands who were members of White Oak Church were often deliberately ignored or unintentionally overlooked when casting prominent roles in plays and programs sponsored by the local schools. Thus church programs at White Oak, such as the Christmas program involving school-age children, placed them in the forefront to act and perform before an assembled congregation. Even so, my friends and I were reluctant participants in activities sponsored by women in the church.

Always held on Christmas Eve, the Christmas program fashioned by the ladies nearly always followed the same format. Typically, there was a Bible reading about the birth of Christ, usually taken from the Gospel of Luke, that was accompanied by a simple play around a manger scene with the characters of Mary, Joseph, the baby Jesus, shepherds, and wise men (all dressed in homemade costumes) who awkwardly portrayed the birth event of Christ. There were recitations and songs by individuals. On one occasion, my mother, who saw values other than religious values in having her children perform in public programs, persuaded me to sing "O Holy Night" as a solo with her accompanying me on the piano. Even for a trained voice this is a difficult song to sing, and for a teenager even more so. But my mother insisted that I sing so I did because I had no choice. Needless to say, it was not an exceptionally good performance and, as I recall, was marked by much snickered whispering and restlessness in an audience already noisily looking forward to the distribution of gifts at the end of the service. J. C. Adcox, Sydney Edwards, J. C. Bennett, Marie Hester, Dorothy Adcox and other childhood friends often muddled through recitations and songs that the congregation mercifully tolerated in the spirit of Christmas. Despite our lack of expertise, church members were always magnanimous in their applause, at times overly so. For it seemed that all the rehearsing that had preceded our performance failed to result in any significant improvement. There was always a sigh of relief when the Christmas play was over because the best part of the evening—the main event from the children's standpoint—was yet to come.

Several weeks before Christmas, the members of each Sunday School class had "drawn" names. Drawing a name obligated a person to provide a gift for the individual whose name he had drawn. Because of the hard times when few church members had money to spend, these gifts, if bought, were usually very inexpensive, usually a handkerchief, a tie, or a pair of socks. More often than not the packages contained homemade items. (Some gifts were even recycled year after year. My father and Uncle Dave Pait kept exchanging the same two ties Christmas after Christmas.) Adding to the anticipation was the secrecy imposed as part of the drawings. No one was suppose to reveal the name that he had drawn. This was to prevent hard feelings toward anyone who failed to provide a gift or whose gift greatly disappointed the recipient. Of course, some people could not keep a secret! As part of the Christmas Eve festivities, the ladies program committee placed a large, highly decorated Christmas tree in the front part of the church well away from the huge pot-bellied stove that when fired glowed a brilliant red and radiated diminishing heat in a broad circle. Piled high around the base of the tree were brightly wrapped packages, some large, some small, that church members brought as a result of the drawing of names.

If the drawing system had worked to perfection, then every person who attended a Sunday School class when names were drawn would both provide and receive a gift. Needless to say, the system did not work perfectly and there were always some adult members of the congregation who attended the Christmas Eve performance who expected but did not receive a gift. Some individuals, who for a range of reasons, simply could neither afford to buy nor were able to make a gift for the person whose they had drawn. However, for the children there was certain to be a gift of candy and fruit. Among the children and teenagers, the sight of all those gifts under the tree created much excitement, especially when one's name was called out by Santa Clause who always arrived to great fanfare. A number of forgotten men played the role of Santa, but the person that I remember as the most outstanding Santa was Warren Hester, my Great-Uncle Jim's son. Warren was a plump young man whose size made him an excellent choice when in costume. The entrance of Santa into the church was the highlight of the evening. He was always met with lots of clapping and shouts of glee from the children who were often surprised that Santa Claus had bothered to come to White Oak Church.

White Oak had an long-practiced system for guaranteeing that every child received a gift following the Christmas Eve program and the distributing of gifts. During the annual church elections, a church member was chosen to be responsible for a small, barrel-shaped bank that each Sunday was to be placed on the altar of the church. Shortly before breaking up into classes following the general assembly, the superintendent of the Sunday School would ask if anyone had celebrated a birthday during the week. If so, according to church custom, that person was expected to donate to the bank one penny for each year of his life. As I recall, nearly every Sunday some member, a child or an adult, walked to the altar and deposited money into the bank, provoking much noisy speculation in the congregation about the person's age. As the year progressed, the little bank gradually filled with coins, sometimes completely, sometimes not. As Christmas approached, the person responsible for keeping the bank met with a few church members, counted the money, and then used it to purchase fruit, nuts and candy to be placed in small paper bags for distribution to the children after the Christmas Eve program. I recall that the year my father was responsible for the little bank, his committee found that it contained about thirty-five dollars when opened. This was in the late thirties and, of course, thirty-five dollars in those difficult times would buy a lot of fruit, nuts and candy. In this way, every child who attended the Christmas Eve service went home carrying a small bag of treats such as fruit, candy, and nuts. In some cases, this was much of what he received for Christmas. In the thirties as a yearly bonus to its workers, the management of the local cotton mills often distributed a sack of fruit, nuts and candy. This was never a guarantee. So the practice of distributing a small sack of goodies continued throughout the thirties and forties while I was remained a member of White Oak Church.

Today it is difficult to imagine how so little of material things brought so much happiness to so many people. The people who streamed into the Christmas Eve service, walking along Highway 211 from the mill villages and nearby residences for the Christmas program, had very little of worldly goods when compared to the people of today. As I recall, only four people in the congregation owned cars—old model cars, at that—Graham Wilson, Sam Edwards, LeRoy Brown and Harry Pait. Nevertheless, despite all the difficulties with the economy of the thirties and the war in the forties, people with little or nothing of worldly goods left these Christmas Eve services renewed in spirit and expectant about tomorrow. At times the members of White Oak were a contentious lot, a condition that probably resulted from so many of them being related to each other by birth or marriage. They argued and fussed about many things, a lot of the disagreements having to do with church matters. However, during the Christmas Eve service, all the hard feelings produced by disputes over family or church issues seemed to be brushed aside, at least for the night. The congregation was joyous throughout the evening, even when the music, recitations, and the play turned out to be less than perfect. For a short while, the cares of the day—stress and uncertainty of work in the mills; poor prices for cotton, tobacco, and corn; concerns about health, the war, etc.—all were temporarily forgotten as the spell of Christmas worked its magic. It is for this reason, that the Christmas Eve service at White Oak Church remains so memorable.

Chapter 13

Memorable Funerals

> . . . For what is your life? It is even vapour that appeareth
> for a little time, and then vanisheth away.

> James 4: 14 KJV

Life and death mark the life of every congregation and that of White
Oak Church was no exception. At a time when life expectancy was not
as long as it is today, the church's membership consisted of a number of
elderly people, especially the children of Daniel and Excie Hester (who
were my mother's aunts and uncles), most of whom were born in the
late nineteenth century. Others in the congregation (for example, Rev.
H. C. Adcox and Graham and Ada Wilson) were of the same generation
as the offsprings of Daniel and Excie. Everyone expected death to occur
among these elderly members from time to time. So much so, that even
among youngsters like myself, there was an awareness that somehow
death and old age were inextricably bound together. Of course, death
among the members of White Oak was not limited to the elderly.
Occasionally death also struck the young, an event that resulted either
from disease or accident. Whether old or young, the death of a member
was traumatic for the congregation, and the resulting funeral at White
Oak was a dramatic event of such widespread sadness and open grief
that it left a lasting impression upon people attending, especially the
young.

Unlike the funeral services of the thirties and forties, funeral services
today are highly sanitized. They appear to be designed to obscure the
finality of death in order to lessened the grief of loved ones. Services
usually occur in a modern "funeral home" where the carefully prepared
body of the deceased lies in a too expensive coffin for viewing by

family and friends during a formal "visitation" lasting perhaps several hours. Whatever grief is evident is usually that of the immediate family of the deceased. Observing the actions and attitudes of the visitors at such visitations, one gets the impression that most have come out of a sense of obligation resulting from an association with the deceased at work, church, or social club and not from genuine love or affection. Rarely does one observe among the visitors a grief expressed in tears or sobbing. Instead, a visitation is an event remarkably similar to a social gathering. A person's death has been simply the means of bringing people together. (Of course, in years past when families were physically separated by distance and rarely saw one another because of inadequate transportation, the death of a family member served the purpose of bringing together widely separated relatives into a necessary reunion marked by misfortune.) And for many people today, mere attendance at the visitation satisfies all obligations to the deceased. There is now no felt obligation to attend the final service, which has become shorter and shorter, usually consisting of a few verses of Scriptures read by a minister, perhaps a canned song provided as part of the service by the funeral director, a few words of praise for the life of the deceased by the minister or family members, words of condolences for the immediate loved ones by the minister, and that is it. Afterwards, the deceased is sent on his way to the grave, followed by the minister, direct family members, and a few friends.

During the thirties and forties, final services at White Oak Church were in sharp contrast to the modern day services described above. There were no funeral "parlors" or "funeral homes" where the deceased lay in state awaiting burial. When a church member died he spent his final hours at his residence, his real home, where someone, family member or friend, was constantly in attendance near his casket through the day and through the night. As a child, I remember my father sitting up in the middle of the night with Tully Singletary, a deceased neighbor, who had lived across the street from us on the Old Mill village. And much later when my mother died, at her request her body lay in state in our family home where she wanted to spend her last hours, and where, incidentally, my Uncle Arthur Suggs had previously lain in state. There were no formal hours of visitation. Friends and neighbors dropped in to bring food and to express their condolences at their convenience, so that there was a constant coming and going of friends and relatives, while the deceased lay nearby in an open casket for viewing. Of course, at this time, the funeral industry was not as it is today. In Bladenboro, Ed Lewis was the local undertaker who was available to provide caskets, which he once kept on the second floor of his furniture store on Front Street, and embalming services. And in nearby Lumberton there was the Biggs funeral establishment that some folks in Bladenboro preferred to use. However, neither provided the kind of standard, glossy services remotely like those provided by today's funeral establishments. To lie in state at home, therefore, was logical, desirable, and certainly cheaper.

The funeral services at White Oak Church were also very different from the often short, formal services that ministers conduct today in modern funeral establishments. At White Oak, services seemed designed to wring every drip of emotion and grief out of everyone—not just family members—but everyone who attended. Furthermore, the ministers who "preached the funeral" of the deceased often exploited their opportunity to evangelize a captive audience, reminding sinners and the unsaved of what awaited them in the hereafter if they failed to seek forgiveness for their errant ways. As family members sat together before an open casket, the preacher, while looking down and over the exposed face of the deceased, frequently alternated between praising all the Christian virtues and good qualities of the dead and issuing threats and warnings of hellfire and damnation to all non-believers who, perhaps unlike the deceased, rejected Christ and refused salvation. It was not uncommon for the funeral sermon to assume the characteristics of sermons one might hear in the Spring or Fall revivals held at the church. And there was a great display of grief. Favorable words from the preacher about the deceased usually provoked loud crying and sobbing from members of the immediate family and close friends who attended. Furthermore, any comments about the loving relationship that the deceased had with a spouse, children, siblings, and other family members also produced much weeping. If the deceased had a favorite hymn, it was sung. If not, the songs were usually "Nearer My God to Thee," "Shall We Gather at the River?," or "Abide with Me." After the preacher had preached and the songs had been sung, the final act of the service was a final viewing of the body. As I recall, those persons in attendance were giving an opportunity for a final walk by the open casket to pay their respects, after, of course, the family members had gathered around the casket for a last viewing and farewell and, after much sobbing and weeping, departed for the final ride to the cemetery. To facilitate an orderly viewing, friends and neighbors usually formed a line on one side of the sanctuary, walked by the deceased, and then left the church.

The final phase of a funeral at White Oak Church took place at one of several local cemeteries located near Bladenboro. This was necessary because when selecting a site for the church, the founders accepted a location adjacent to Bryant Swamp, not a suitable place for burials because of the high water table and frequent flooding. Consequently, unlike many churches in the area, White Oak Church never established its own churchyard cemetery. Nevertheless, there were several well-known cemeteries nearby from which family members of White Oak Church chose as the final resting place for a loved one. The most prominent one was the Bridger Cemetery (now known as Pinecrest Cemetery) that is located south of town, a short distance west of the Bladenboro Public Schools. A number of the leading members of the church, including a founder or two, were buried there. My great grandparents Daniel and Exie Hester rest there, as well as some of their children—Maryanne, Rachel, Jim, and other Hesters and their families who made up the church's core membership. Ultimately, my mother and father, who were long-time, early members of White Oak Church, would be buried there. Other prominent members elected to be buried at Oak Grove Original Free Will Baptist Church's cemetery that is located four or five miles north of town off the Dublin road. Among these were Graham and Ada Wilson, two of the most beloved members of the congregation. Roy and Ruby Davis also rest there with their son Fred who, unfortunately, was killed by a car in the Fall of 1940. And my Grandma Fannie Edwards, who died of a stroke at age forty-nine, was also buried there. Located in the "sand hills" south of Bladenboro and off the Evergreen road is another cemetery where some members of White Oak Church elected to be buried, for example, my Aunt Marybelle Pait and her husband Dave. And some chose as their final resting place the Singletary Cemetery near the small town of Butters, not far from Bladenboro, located on a rise adjacent to the Big Swamp.

With so few cars in the congregation, the number of individuals attending a funeral at White Oak Church who then accompanied the immediate family, relatives and pallbearers to the burial site was small. However, sometimes extraordinary measures were taken to provide transportation. When Tully Singletary, a mill hand who lived in a rented house across the street from our family on the Old Mill Village, died in the early thirties, fifteen or twenty individuals, including my father and me, road on a flat bed truck to the Singletary Cemetery in Butters for Tully's interment. It was an experience as a small boy that I shall never forget. But despite the lack of transportation among the members at White Oak Church, I don't recall that there was ever a burying when part of the congregation boarded a flat truck to the grave site. Flat beds were used, although rarely, by the church for other functions (for example, a journey by members of the congregation, including my father and me, to the Free Will Baptist Orphanage in Middlesex) but never to transport church members to a funeral. Nevertheless, despite the problem of transportation, the several grave side rites that I attended while a member of White Oak Church always had people other than family members present.

Regardless of where the deceased was buried, the ritual rarely changed. With family members sitting near the suspended coffin in chairs provided by the funeral director, and with friends and relatives standing nearby, the minister read a few verses of Scripture, made a few additional, comforting comments to the family, added a statement about "ashes to ashes and dust to dust," and ended the service with a brief prayer. In these early funerals of deceased members of White Oak Church that I attended, the pallbearers then lowered the casket of the deceased into box enclosure that would then be sealed with a wooden cover. As I recall, they and other friends and relatives then shoveled dirt onto the box, filling the grave. Friends were sometimes called upon for such service, even the digging of the grave. As a young man, my father and several friends volunteered to dig the grave of a mill worker whose family was financially hard pressed by the difficult times. Attending the burial of Tully Singletary as a small boy, my first funeral, the thumping sound of the dirt when hitting the wooden box in which Tully's coffin lay—it was a terrible, haunting sound—created a memory that has lasted a lifetime. In contrast with a present-day burying, the minister's usually brief remarks concludes the service and after family members have received his condolences and that of the mourners, everyone—including family members—departs, leaving the task of actual burial to a crew of men hired by the funeral home. Today, family members usually do not remain to see a loved one lowered into the ground, which is certainly a humane difference from the old ways.

The congregation of White Oak Church was like its counterparts everywhere in that it was cross generational. Within such a groups, death was a natural occurrence, particularly among the elderly members who were more vulnerable to disease and who, because they lived in a small rural community with doctors but no hospital facilities, did not have immediate access to the best medical care found elsewhere. As for youngsters in the congregation, their deaths were usually the result of accidents. For example, on Highway 211 on which White Oak Church was located, there were five youngsters killed by cars within a period of fifteen years, two of them children of church members—a son of Rev. H. C. and Hattie Adcox and a son of Roy and Ruby Davis. Another child whose parents—Cecil and Dora Bennett—were church members was accidentally shot to death by a friend in his home fronting Highway 211. So death touched all generations in the church. Even so, the death of three members of White Oak are extremely memorable to me.

The first of these deaths was a family member, Great-Grandma Excie Hester, who was the matriarch of the largest family in the church. Following the death of her husband Daniel in March 1936, Grandma Excie moved in with her daughter Rachel Shipman, husband Leland, and their three children—Leo, James, and Vivian. The Shipmans lived in a small house that fronted Highway 211 and near White Oak Church. For several years prior to her death, weather permitting, Grandma Excie sat in a rocker with her cane near the edge of the Shipmans' front porch, dipping snuff and occasionally leaning forward on her cane to spit off the porch. For hours she sat there observing traffic and anyone walking the highway and, if one was headed toward town, she would invariably ask in a high pitched voice, "Are you goin' to the 'Boro?" a question designed to stop the walker in order to talk a spell. She was a feisty, irascible old lady who let it be known early on that when she "passed" and went to be with Daniel and her Lord, she wanted no crying and weeping. After she died on a very cold day in November, her descendants followed her wishes.

On the night that she lay in state in her former bedroom at daughter Rachel's house, the numerous members of Grandma Excie's family were in and out, gathering throughout the night in an adjacent room and clustering for warmth around a red hot heater constantly stoked by grandchildren. As she had directed, sadness was at a minimum. She wanted no "bawling" at her passing because she was ready to meet her "maker." Grandma Excie's death brought home relatives who lived elsewhere in places like St. Pauls and who had not seen each other after a long separation. Consequently, despite Grandma's corpse lying across the hall in her bedroom, members of the family regaled each other with story after story, most of them humorous, about episodes in the life of the deceased. For awhile, the sad reason that had brought them together was mostly forgotten. I suspect that the reunion-like atmosphere was exactly what Grandma Excie wanted. Occasionally, a family member would slip from the room and visit "Ma" or "Grandma" across the hall in a room that was dimly and eerily lit by a single light bulb at the end of a drop cord dangling from the ceiling. But otherwise, the gathering was anything but one overwhelmed by grief. Even so, I am certain that there was unexpressed sadness that was not evident that night. It was impossible to be related to and to know this colorful old woman without feeling an awful sadness at her passing. As a teenager en route to town who had been stopped often with her question from the front porch, "Are you goin' to the 'Boro?" I personally felt great sorrow at her death.

Grandma Excie's funeral at White Oak Church brought together a large crowd of people, most of them direct descendants, who filled the church. Of course, because family members composed the bulk of the congregation, their presence assured that most pews would be filled. The inside service was typical, following that outlined above. Although Grandma Excie had asked that there be no bawling at her funeral, this request was not granted. She had been such an integral part of the extended Hester family, especially since her husband Daniel's death and while she lived with daughter Rachel, that the very thought of her being forever gone provoked outbursts of grief during the course of the funeral. The service at White Oak Church was longer than most because two ministers were involved and because there was such a large number attending. But, after the final viewing of the body, Grandma Excie was taken out to Bridgers Cemetery where she was laid to rest next to her beloved Daniel. Although the cemetery was less than two miles from the church, I did not attend the grave-side ceremony. However, over the years when visiting Bladenboro, I have visited the grave site of Daniel and Excie, two great-grandparents whose extended family that included my mother had so much to do with the history White Oak Church.

To me the second most memorable funeral at White Oak Church was that of Fred Davis, son of Roy and Ruby Davis who were longtime members of the congregation. Because Roy and my mother were both grandchildren of Daniel and Excie Hester, they were first cousins, which made Fred and me second cousins. Fred and I were not only cousins, we were also good friends and sixth-grade classmates in the Bladenboro Elementary School in 1941. Shortly after the start of school in September, 1941 while walking in early evening along Highway 211 with another cousin, Fred darted onto the highway where he was struck by a speeding car and killed instantly. The impact tossed Fred's body directly in front of Leland and Rachel Shipman's home. The Shipman's were aunt and uncle to Roy and my mother.

When this horrible accident occurred, my mother and I were at home, which fronted Highway 211, and heard the frightening screech of brakes followed by a loud thump when the car struck Fred. We knew instantly that someone had been hit by a vehicle. Thinking that the person struck might be my younger brother Charles who had not returned from visiting my Aunt Clara Tyler, who also lived near the highway, my mother sent me to investigate. Racing up the road to the crumpled body, I arrived simultaneously with Bob Hester, another of Roy's uncles who lived directly across the road from the Shipmans. Much to my relief, I realized that it was not my brother Charles but, instead, I sadly recognized my close friend Fred. From the awful wound on Fred's head, even in the growing darkness, it was clear that Fred was dead. I raced home to tell my mother that the victim was not Charles. A crowd gathered in the growing darkness awaiting a local doctor who, when he came, pronounced Fred dead. His body was then placed on the bed of a pickup truck with his father and taken home to await a hearse from nearby Lumberton.

Fred's death was a terrible blow not only to his parents and friends but to the entire White Oak congregation. Like myself, he was not only a youngster in the church; he was part of the Hester clan that composed much of the membership. Consequently, his passing directly touched dozens of relatives. His death was especially hard for me. Never had death been so close and personal. To have a close friend taken so suddenly and violently was a shock that lingered for days. I don't think that afterwards I ever again took life for granted. Fred lay in state at home on the Old Mill village where relatives, friends, and fellow mill workers of Roy and Ruby's flooded the house bringing food and offering condolences. At his funeral, the church was packed with people who wept openly in a great outpouring of grief at the tragedy that had occurred. As a result of my own grief, I remember very little about the formalities of the service. Except for my awareness of the widespread anguish by those attending the "preaching" of the funeral sermon, even today, decades later, the entire service remains a blur for me.

Fred was interred in the cemetery behind Oak Grove Original Free Will Baptist Church. Because of my friendship with Fred and my parents close relationship with Roy and Ruby, somehow our family managed to attend the grave side services. Without a car, we obviously rode to the cemetery with someone; however, I have no idea who provided the transportation. The brief service at the grave was another nerve racking experience for me. Fred's parents were inconsolable, as well as all the relatively few relatives and family friends who had the means of traveling out to Oak Grove Church. Occasionally when visiting the Bladenboro area, I visit the cemetery where Fred and now, Roy and Ruby, are buried. It is also the site where my Grandma Fannie Hester Edwards is buried, and the burial site of other people, such as Graham Wilson, who strongly influenced my life. I never visit Fred's grave without feeling again the terrible, agonizing sense of loss that I felt as a youngster while watching this friend being lowered into the grave. And I find it extremely difficult to suppress images of distraught Roy and Ruby desperately struggling to understand and accept the loss of their son.

For me the third most memorable funeral at White Oak Church occurred several years later when I was a teenager. Graham Wilson, who ran the men's dry goods department in the Bridger Corporation Store, became ill sometime in 1945 (I think) and was sent up to Duke University Hospital in Durham for diagnosis. After running through a battery of test, doctors concluded that he had terminal stomach/ esophageal cancer. He was admitted to the hospital and never returned home alive, dying in August, 1945.

News of the nature of his illness and later his death shocked the congregation and the entire town of Bladenboro. For years Wilson and his wife Ada had been mainstays in the church, serving in nearly all offices. They were a very devout couple whose daughter Marie, a missionary, was even then, as I recall, abroad somewhere in South America. Like everyone else in the church, my parents greatly admired and respected the Wilsons because of the kind of people they were. In their opinion, the Wilsons exemplified what the Christian life should be. As for me, at the time of his death, I already had a number of youthful memories associated with the man I then called "Mr. Graham." As a very small boy, I remember riding in the rumble seat of his Ford Model A with my father on trips to Durham so that my mother could visit the Duke clinic for an analyses of a heart condition. Having one of the few cars in the congregation, Wilson generously took days off from clerking at the Bridger Corporation to make those trips. And when I was in my early teens, "Mr. Graham" took me fishing out to Singletary's and Nance's millponds on Wednesday afternoons. (At one time, the whole town shut down on Wednesday afternoon to compensate clerks who were expected to work late into Saturday night.) At the time, my father was commuting and working in the wartime shipyards in Wilmington and, as a result, he had little time for fishing with his son. "Mr. Graham" was generous with his time and was very helpful to my family in some very rough times.

Wilson's funeral at White Oak Church was unlike that of my friend Fred Davis whose service attracted principally family and church members. As a clerk at the leading mercantile establishment in Bladenboro, Wilson knew nearly everyone in the immediate area. And because of the type of man that he was, he was much admired and respected by scores of people. Consequently, his funeral service attracted many persons outside the White Oak Church family. And unlike Fred's service that provoked an enormous outpouring of emotion because of his youth, his family connections, and the tragic nature of his death, Wilson's service—although certainly filled with sadness not only among direct family members but for others who knew him—did not produce the same level of visual grief. Except for immediate members of the family, the people attending were more restrained in their outward display of emotions. As I recall, the number of people attending the service was swollen because out of respect for Wilson, most of the stores in town had closed as a way of honoring the man. A lot of these people attended not only Wilson's church service but also his burial rites at the cemetery.

As noted previously, the family elected to bury "Mr. Graham" in the cemetery at Oak Grove Original Free Will Baptist Church. At the time of his death, I was a Boy Scout belonging to Troop 72 under the direction of Rev. Benjamin Ormand, pastor of the Presbyterian Church in Bladenboro. Because a large number of people were expected to follow the hearse out to Oak Grove Church, and because the winding country roads into the church grounds off the Dublin highway were narrow and unpaved, Rev. Orman volunteered the Scouts from Troop 72 to help in directing traffic and showing people where to park in the small area around the church. Partly because of this duty but principally because "Mr. Graham" was such a good friend to me and my family, I remember his death and funeral as one of the most memorable that I observed while a member of White Oak Church. He was a good, generous, and honest man who greatly influenced my life.

Of course, there were many other funerals that occurred at White Oak Church during my youth, but the three noted above were the ones that stand out vividly in my memory. After I left for college, military service, and marriage, my life as a member of the church was virtually over. Close relatives—aunts, uncles, and cousins who were church members—died after I had established residence elsewhere, and although I heard about their passing, I was not able to be present for their services. Furthermore, during the late fifties there was another disconnect from the church. For a variety of reasons, my parents became unhappy and dissatisfied at White Oak Church and transferred their membership over to the First Baptist Church of Bladenboro located on what was then called Front Street. As it turned out, despite all the family roots existing at their former church, the move to First Baptist turned out to be a blessing because they were very happy there until their deaths. However, their change of membership meant that when I visited them in Bladenboro, the family worshiped at First Baptist, not White Oak, the church whose members were such an important part of my youth.

POSTSCRIPT

After composing and rereading these vignettes of my youthful years as part of White Oak Original Free Will Baptist Church, I was surprised at how vivid my memories are of the people who made up the congregation. I should not have been! From the time of my birth to adulthood, I was a part of the membership (most of whom were aunts, uncles, and cousins of my mother) both in and out of the church. Consequently, it was inevitable that the influence on me of church members would be strong and pervasive. It was also inevitable that growing up in the church, my early perception of the world would be seen through the lens of the Free Will Baptists. Furthermore, the restrictions of the times augmented that influence. Other than White Oak Church, there were only two other institutions that came close to equaling its influence on my youth, and they were my family and the local public schools.

Because the times imposed limitations for personal growth outside the church, these three institutions—church, family and school—very much determined the major dimensions of my character. As has been noted, very few of White Oak's congregation had automobiles, so that the opportunities to travel beyond Bladenboro and view the world from a different perspective were few and far between for most of White Oak's young people. For example, until leaving home for Wake Forest College (now University) in the Fall of 1947, my personal travel outside Bladenboro had been only to "far away" places like Raleigh (to the State Fair), to Charlotte (as part of the Whiteville American Legion Baseball team), to Winston Salem (as a member of the high school Beta Club), and to Wilmington (to work in a kiosk outside the Wilmington shipyard during World War II). Until becoming a part of the armed forces, my only out-of-state travel was to Myrtle Beach, SC. My limited experience of travel was typical, I think, of most of the town's youngsters. Unlike today's teenagers who often roam over faraway places through the United States and abroad, during the thirties and forties I and other youngsters of White Oak Church traveled infrequently and not far from home. Of course, that further increased the impact that the church had on our lives.

The doctrines of the Free Will Baptist denomination also imposed limitations on personal growth outside the church. For example, there were certain kinds of activities that Free Will Baptist parents discouraged—even prohibited—their children from doing. Although these limitations were not nearly as restrictive as some of the more evangelical denominations, they nevertheless were confining. At the time I was growing up within the denomination, Free Will Baptists, certainly many of those belonging to White Oak Church, taught their children that attending movies, or "picture shows," was a "sin" and should be avoided. It did not matter how innocent the theme of the movie might be, they were corrupting to the point of endangering one's eternal soul. Fortunately, my parents did not feel this strongly about the Saturday matinee of western movies that was the standard fare at the Lyric (later the Wonet) theater in town.

Dancing was also considered a taboo. Of course, in Bladenboro there was not much chance of a young person in White Oak Church falling into this trap. Unlike today when schools sponsor dances regularly, throughout my entire public school career I don't recall ever attending a school sponsored dance. If one wished to dance, it was necessary to visit White Lake, nearly twenty miles away, where dances were held in the Hay Loft on Saturday nights, or, travel to Lake Wacamaw and visit the Anchorage, which had a juke box and dance floor. There was no such place in Bladenboro. Other activities such as playing cards and shooting pool at Pelo's pool hall were frowned upon as corrupting influences on one's morals. The young people of White Oak, especially its young males, were encouraged to avoid these activities. Of course, Pelo Lockamy's pool emporium was a big temptation that many of us could not resist even though a visit there was likely to be quickly reported to parents. And although the young people of the church heard a lot of profanity—even by some of its members—foul language was strongly discouraged. Alcohol beverages—hard liquor, wine and beer—were absolutely prohibited, although it was common knowledge that certain members of the church enjoyed the beverage obtained from nearby bootleggers. Despite these admonitions and efforts on the part of the church to channel the character of its young people in the

Christian way, by the time of our late teens many of us had violated at least a few of these strictures. It was impossible during the uncertain times of the war years for the youth of the church not to be affected in negative ways by all the changes and turmoil then wracking society. Teenage boys, who fully expected to be drafted into the armed forces upon turning eighteen, often were daring in violating their parents' admonitions. The war and the looming draft influenced our attitudes and behavior about many things.

Even so, the influence of White Oak Church upon its young people during the hectic depression years of the thirties and the tumultuous war years of the early forties was profound. Most of us who grew up in the church during that era were molded substantially by that institution and its members. As for me, I say that with certainty. Those early years at White Oak helped to shape me and partly make me who I am. This was true even of those few members whose actions within and outside the church caused me to view them somewhat negatively. There were many, many good Christian people who touched my life in those years. I was blessed within the church with many relatives—aunts, uncles, cousins—and though from time to time I viewed them critically, I remember them all with love and affection. They were among the best people that I have ever known.